MACMILLAN MASTER GUIDES

GENERAL EDITOR: JAMES GIBSON

JANE AUSTEN	*Emma* Norman Page
	Sense and Sensibility Judy Simons
	Persuasion Judy Simons
	Pride and Prejudice Raymond Wilson
	Mansfield Park Richard Wirdnam
SAMUEL BECKETT	*Waiting for Godot* Jennifer Birkett
WILLIAM BLAKE	*Songs of Innocence and Songs of Experience* Alan Tomlinson
ROBERT BOLT	*A Man for All Seasons* Leonard Smith
CHARLOTTE BRONTË	*Jane Eyre* Robert Miles
EMILY BRONTË	*Wuthering Heights* Hilda D. Spear
GEOFFREY CHAUCER	*The Miller's Tale* Michael Alexander
	The Pardoner's Tale Geoffrey Lester
	The Wife of Bath's Tale Nicholas Marsh
	The Knight's Tale Anne Samson
	The Prologue to the Canterbury Tales Nigel Thomas and Richard Swan
JOSEPH CONRAD	*The Secret Agent* Andrew Mayne
CHARLES DICKENS	*Bleak House* Dennis Butts
	Great Expectations Dennis Butts
GEORGE ELIOT	*Middlemarch* Graham Handley
	Silas Marner Graham Handley
	The Mill on the Floss Helen Wheeler
T. S. ELIOT	*Selected Poems* Andrew Swarbrick
HENRY FIELDING	*Joseph Andrews* Trevor Johnson
E. M. FORSTER	*Howards End* Ian Milligan
WILLIAM GOLDING	*The Spire* Rosemary Sumner
	Lord of the Flies Raymond Wilson
OLIVER GOLDSMITH	*She Stoops to Conquer* Paul Ranger
THOMAS HARDY	*The Mayor of Casterbridge* Ray Evans
	Tess of the d'Urbervilles James Gibson
BEN JONSON	*Volpone* Michael Stout
JOHN KEATS	*Selected Poems* John Garrett
PHILIP LARKIN	*The Whitsun Weddings* and *The Less Deceived* Andrew Swarbrick
D.H. LAWRENCE	*Sons and Lovers* R. P. Draper
HARPER LEE	*To Kill a Mockingbird* Jean Armstrong
GERARD MANLEY HOPKINS	*Selected Poems* R. J. C. Watt
CHRISTOPHER MARLOWE	*Doctor Faustus*

MACMILLAN MASTER GUIDES

THE METAPHYSICAL POETS Joan van Emden

THOMAS MIDDLETON and *The Changeling* Tony Bromham
WILLIAM ROWLEY

ARTHUR MILLER *The Crucible* Leonard Smith
Death of a Salesman Peter Spalding

GEORGE ORWELL *Animal Farm* Jean Armstrong

WILLIAM SHAKESPEARE *Richard II* Charles Barber
Othello Tony Bromham
Hamlet Jean Brooks
King Lear Francis Casey
Henry V Peter Davison
The Winter's Tale Diana Devlin
Julius Caesar David Elloway
Macbeth David Elloway
The Merchant of Venice A. M. Kinghorn
Measure for Measure Mark Lilly
Henry IV Part I Helen Morris
Romeo and Juliet Helen Morris
A Midsummer Night's Dream
  Kenneth Pickering
The Tempest Kenneth Pickering
Coriolanus Gordon Williams
Antony and Cleopatra Martin Wine
Twelfth Night R. P. Draper

RICHARD SHERIDAN *The School for Scandal* Paul Ranger
The Rivals Jeremy Rowe

EDWARD THOMAS *Selected Poems* Gerald Roberts

JOHN WEBSTER *The White Devil* and *The Duchess of Malfi*
  David A. Male

VIRGINIA WOOLF *To the Lighthouse* John Mepham
Mrs Dalloway Julian Pattison

MACMILLAN MASTER GUIDES

HOWARDS END

BY E. M. FORSTER

IAN MILLIGAN

Published by
PALGRAVE MACMILLAN
Houndmills, Basingstoke, Hampshire RG21 6XS and
175 Fifth Avenue, New York, N. Y. 10010
Companies and representatives throughout the world

PALGRAVE MACMILLAN is the global academic imprint of the Palgrave
Macmillan division of St. Martin's Press, LLC and of Palgrave Macmillan Ltd.
Macmillan® is a registered trademark in the United States, United Kingdom
and other countries. Palgrave is a registered trademark in the European
Union and other countries.

ISBN 0–333–41675–9 paperback

This book is printed on paper suitable for recycling and made from fully
managed and sustained forest sources.

A catalogue record for this book is available from the British Library.

Printed and bound in Great Britain by
Antony Rowe Ltd, Chippenham and Eastbourne

CONTENTS

GENERAL EDITOR'S PREFACE

The aim of the Macmillan Master Guides is to help you to appreciate the book you are studying by providing information about it and by suggesting ways of reading and thinking about it that will lead to fuller understanding. The section on the writer's life and background have been designed to illustrate those aspects of the writer's life which have influenced the work, and to place it in its personal and literary context. The summaries and critical commentary are of special importance in that each brief summary of the action is followed by an examination of the significant critical points. The space which might have been given to repetitive explanatory notes has been devoted to a detailed analysis of the kind of passage which might confront you in an examination. Literary criticism is concerned with both the broader aspects of the work being studied and with its detail. The ideas which meet us in reading a great work of literature, and their relevance to us today, are an essential part of our study, and our Guides look at the thought of their subject in some detail. But just as essential is the craft with which the writer has constructed his work of art, and this may be considered under several technical headings – characterisation, language, style and stagecraft, for example.

The authors of these Guides are all teachers and writers of wide experience, and they have chosen to write about books they admire and know well in the belief that they can communicate their admiration to you. But you yourself must read and know intimately the book you are studying. No one can do that for you. You should see this book as a lamp-post. Use it to shed light, not to lean against. If you know your text and know what it is saying about life, and how it says it, then you will enjoy it, and there is no better way of passing an examination in literature.

JAMES GIBSON

Acknowledgement

Cover illustration: *Women Seated in a Garden* by Toulouse-Lautrec. Reported by Courtesy of the Trustees, The National Gallery, London.

1 THE MAN AND HIS WORK

Edward Morgan Forster was born in London in 1879. His mother, Lily Winchelo, was a young woman of intelligence and character, who had been befriended by a well-to-do spinster connected with a famous group of philanthropic Evangelical Christians called 'The Clapham Sect'. His father, the nephew of Lily's benefactress, died soon after his son was born. After living with various friends, Forster's mother took him to live in a house called 'Rooksnest' in Stevenage, Hertfordshire. The description of 'Howards End' in the first chapter of the novel is closely based on 'Rooksnest'. It, too, had a meadow, a vine and a wych-elm into the bark of which were stuck 'three or four fangs', according to Forster's later account. Forster was a precocious and imaginative child, closely attached to his lively mother. Apart from a succession of garden boys, who were his childhood playmates, he grew up in a household of women.

After he had spent some years in a preparatory school at Eastbourne, his mother moved to Tonbridge in Kent so that he could attend Tonbridge School as a day-boy. There he studied classics and was interested in music, art and literature. Although he did not enjoy his school-days, he had some academic success and won a place at King's College, Cambridge, in 1896. There he gradually made friends and became a member of discussion groups whose members were sceptical and open-minded. He began to lose his belief in Christianity. By his third year in Cambridge he had established himself as in an intelligent but rather whimsical man of wide intellectual sympathies, his reading embracing the whole of classical and modern English literature. He was liberal and anti-imperialist at a time when the war against the Boers in South Africa generated much militaristic feeling in Britain. He graduated in 1900 with a degree in classics but was able to study history for a further year on the strength of a College Scholarship. In that year he was elected to the 'Apostles', a distinguished, if secretive, Cambridge discussion group which combined friendship and the pursuit of truth. Among its leading members at this time were G. E. Moore, the philospher, G. H. Hardy, the mathematician, and, a close friend of Forster's at the time, H. O. Meredith, who later became a professor of economics at Belfast. Forster was impressed with his self-confidence and good looks, and it was through his friendship with Meredith that he came to recognise his own homosexuality.

Forster had been left money by his mother's benefactress, so that he did not immediately need to pursue a career. His academic attainments were not thought good enough for him to hope for a fellowship at Cambridge, but he had made a first attempt to begin writing a novel. He chose to visit Italy with his mother, intending to equip himself to become an extra-mural lecturer in art or Italian history. While he was there, he wrote his first short story. By 1904 Forster and his mother were living in London. He had begun to contribute to a new monthly called *The Independent Review* and he had begun work on a novel based on his Italian experiences, which was the embryo of *A Room With a View*. He had begun to do some extra-mural teaching for Cambridge; he taught in the Working Men's College in London, and he had been asked to produce an edition of Virgil's *Aeneid*. He began to explore the English landscape on a number of walking-tours, and had an encounter with a young shepherd boy near Salisbury which was incorporated into the material for a novel which he had sketched out in the summer of 1904 and which developed into *The Longest Journey*. By the end of 1904 he had in hand three novels and some short stories. He felt dissatisfied, however, because he had no regular work; at the suggestion of a friend he went to Germany as tutor to the children of an Australian writer who had married a German count. At the same time his first novel – *Where Angels Fear to Tread* – was accepted for publication.

After his return to England in 1906 he was asked to tutor an Indian boy, Syed Ross Masood, who was about to go to Oxford. He was the grandson of a famous Muslim educationalist, but he had been brought up in England. Forster and he became close friends and it was from this friendship that Forster's interest in India developed. In 1907 Forster's second novel, *The Longest Journey*, was published. It is the most autobiographical of his novels; its early chapters reflects some aspects of his life at Cambridge. It is also Forster's most trenchant attack on the meanness of spirit which he found so stifling in English middle-class life. In 1908 his third novel, *A Room with a View*, was published. Although Forster was dissatisfied with it, it has a brilliant lightness of tone and a sympathetic heroine who, though surrounded by the orthodox English society described in his earlier novels, manages to escape to a life of happiness with a spontaneously affectionate young man, not quite of her own class.

Literary success brought Forster into contact with a wider world. He began to associate with the 'Bloomsbury Group' of writers and artists brought together by the daughters of a well-known Victorian literary man, Leslie Stephen, one of whom was later to become famous as the novelist, Virginia Woolf. Now he began to work on his next novel, *Howards End*, drawing for some of his material on the people he had met at the Working Man's College. Some parts of the novel – the account of Helen's seduction, in particular – caused adverse comment among its first readers, not, as might be expected, on the grounds of its implausibility but because it was considered improper. But the novel was in general greeted as the work of a significant new writer whose literary reputation was now established.

In 1912 he left with two friends for his first visit to India. Although he greatly enjoyed this experience, much of which he later used in *A Passage to India*, he found it difficult to complete a new novel he had begun in 1911. Forster had come to believe that he could not write more novels about relationships between men and women. He wrote a novel called *Maurice* about homosexual relationships, but he knew that this and other short stories on this theme could not be published.

On the outbreak of war in 1914, he first considered joining an ambulance unit in Italy but finally went to work for the Red Cross in Egypt, where he remained until the end of the war. When he returned to England in 1919 he worked for the government in various capacities, then became a journalist. He had come to think that his career as novelist was over. In 1921 he went back to India to work for the ruler of the State of Dewas. The following year he returned to England, having begun work on a new novel, which was to become *A Passage to India*, published in 1924. In 1926 he was invited to give the Clark Lectures at Trinity College, Cambridge: they were afterwards published as *Aspects of the Novel*. As a result of their success he was offered a three-year fellowship at King's College. In later years Forster was known as a writer and broadcaster, who had a strong interest in public affairs. Two collections of his essays, reviews and broadcast talks, *Abinger Harvest* and *Two Cheers for Democracy*, were published in 1936 and 1951. Although his reputation as a novelist grew, he wrote no more novels. After the Second World War he was invited to live in King's College, Cambridge. He lived there until the end of his life, writing no more novels but producing, in 1953 *The Hill of Devi*, an account of his experiences in India, and in 1956 *Marianne Thornton*, a biography of his great-aunt. After his death in 1970 a long-unpublished noel *Maurice* on the theme of homosexuality was published.

2 READING *HOWARDS END*

Howards End is not an easy novel to understand unless the reader begins to notice the trail of clues Forster has laid to guide him. In his book, *Aspects of the Novel*, (1927) Forster distinguished 'the story' from 'the novel', explaining that these two elements of a work of fiction correspond to two components of everyday life. In the second chapter of his book he says:

> daily life, whatever it may be really, is practically composed of two lives – the life in time and the life in values – and our conduct reveals a double allegiance. 'I only saw her for five minutes, but it was worth it'. There you have both allegiances in a simple sentence. And what the story does is to narrate the life in time. And what the entire novel does – if it is a good novel – is to include the life by values as well; using devices hereafter to be examined.

Some novelists have attended to the second of these elements of fiction by intervening directly to tell their readers what their characters think and what their readers should think too. Other novelists, like Forster, have preferred a more indirect approach. They want to involve the reader more actively in the interpretation of the novel. They do not intervene in the action with direct commentary; they allow events to unfold before the eyes of their readers who are expected to make their own assessment of the actions of the characters. As the reader will soon discover, Forster is not completely detached from the novel. There is a narrative commentary which is sometimes extensive. There are two points to notice about it: first, it is often difficult to pin down. The narrative voice is sometimes oblique, evasive or ironic, so that the reader must pause for a moment to judge its tone and take stock of its meaning. The second point is that the narrative voice sometimes merges imperceptibly into the inner thoughts of the character from whose point of view the story is being told. The reader has to be careful to distinguish statements and comments which are made with the full authority of the narrator from statements of belief and judgement made by individual characters, which are open to consideration by the reader.

Exploring the world of values is a complex operation. In the lives that they live through time, characters discover and create values. Their choice of friends or lovers or pursuits or jobs indicates the values to which they are committed. Of course, these values may change. Characters may discover that they have made the wrong choices. The interest of the novel will lie in following their courses of action to see what principles of action they discover and how they distinguish right decisions from wrong, desirable from undesirable courses of action.

But in allowing the reader freedom to follow the action with relatively little overt authorial guidance, Forster is careful to offer guidance of a less obvious kind. He does this by constructing patterns within the material of the novel which may steer the reader towards an interpretation of it which is in accordance with the novelist's own view. In *Howards End* Forster tells a story which has many conventional features: in the 'life of time' his characters form plans and undertake actions which have happy or unhappy consequences. At a simple level the reader is invited to consider these actions and decisions from the point of view of their 'success', although it may not be so simple to judge why they are successful, or if they are. Characters may be grouped together and compared with one another so that different ways of life or reasons for action can be looked at carefully and critically. Looked at from this point of view, the action of a novel consists in a process of complication followed by one of simplification and clarification. Contrasting groups of characters are set in motion; their conflicting actions reveal the principles which they habitually use, whether they know it or not; and by the outcomes he devises for each train of events or group of characters, the author reveals his own values and persuades us to consider our own.

Just as the author may contrast the actions of the characters so that they come to form a pattern which indirectly expresses the values of the author, so too may the places in which the action takes place. Setting may express preference or value so that, for example, 'town' is opposed to 'country'. In *Howards End* the values of the characters find expression in how they think of their houses: Wickham Place is contrasted with Ducie Street; Oniton Grange is a stepping stone to Howards End. Forster is able to invest places with sudden unexpected significance so that King's Cross Station is momentarily something more than a station and St Paul's Cathedral is something less than a church. The Six Hills, which are the graves of Danish soldiers, are repeatedly used to refer to values established by history; the vine and the wych-elm of Howards End gradually acquire associations which are offered for the reader's approval during the course of the novel.

Patterns of a similar kind may even be worked into the texture of the words the author uses to tell his story. Consider, for example, the repeated use of the word 'grey' to suggest everything that stifles and represses spontaneity and expressiveness, everything that encourages conformity and routine. Or think of Forster's use of the words 'collide' and 'collision' when he wants to speak of the chance events which bring the characters of the novel together as opposed to the word 'connect' which Forster uses when the characters are able to see some sense in these encounters or to make something significant out of them. There are many words which Forster uses in a similar way to establish the 'rhythm' of his novel – an expression he uses himself for the pattern in time which is set up when a reader begins to notice these repetitions in the process of reading the novel. Forster calls this method of composition 'repetition with variation'.

Forster treats other paired words in a similar way. They are usually abstract words whose meaning is not wholly clear-cut. The repetition is not the dull duplication of some simple concept, though perhaps his repeated motifs may be criticised because they are not explicit enough, leaving their meaning too open to the interpretation of the reader. We can think of such terms as 'the seen' and 'the unseen', 'the beast' and 'the monk', 'the warp' and 'the woof' of life – money being the first of these, other things ('culture', perhaps) being the second. All of these phrases have to be placed at some point on the familiar line which runs between 'the material' and 'the spiritual'. What the first set of terms means is clear enough: money, houses, possessions, sex, family, economy and empire are all words which would find a convenient place at one end of the scale. It might be more difficult to suggest the terms which would be appropriate for the other: friendship, loyalty, honesty, a love of natural things and a concern for their preservation, a desire to see all the aspects of life as part of a unified whole. Some of these qualities might appear at the 'spiritual' end of the scale. There would be a place for music, though none, apparently, for God. The position of books appears uncertain.

Perhaps one reason for Forster's use of vagueness is that he is engaged in re-ordering and re-arranging our ideas of what is spiritually significant. It is perfectly reasonable for him to do so, but the reader should be alert to the fact that such a revaluation is going on. It is surely right not to be too easily persuaded to look at life in Forster's way. Another range of repeated words seems to refer to concepts which are not subject to revaluation in this way. Words such as 'Infinity', 'Death', 'Love', 'Joy' seem to point to more general themes of human experience or human speculation. 'Love' and 'Joy' suggest the positive pole of human experience, 'Death' the negative. 'Infinity' suggests the mystery which surrounds any attempt to unite them in a meaningful way. 'Only connect' is the epigraph of the novel, but what is to be connected and does such an event take place in the course of the novel? Reading *Howards End* with an alertness to the contrasts and oppositions which Forster has established at the level of character, setting, theme, and language will help the reader to decide whether he has found a pattern which convincingly resolves these questions.

3 SUMMARIES AND CRITICAL COMMENTARY

CHAPTER 1

Summary

In a letter to her sister Margaret, Helen Schlegel writes from Howards End to describe the house and the Wilcox family who own it. The house is old and large, covered with a vine, set among trees, with a wych-elm apparently overhanging it. Helen had not expected it to be so simple because the Wilcoxes were rich and perhaps a little ostentatious. Margaret has had to stay at home with their brother, Tibby, who has hay-fever. Charles Wilcox has hay-fever too, but he is brave about it. Helen describes Mrs Wilcox as she tends her garden, unaffected by the hay, whereas Charles and his father have begun to sneeze. Three days later Helen writes again to say how happy she is with the Wilcoxes, even if they do not have her advanced views. Mr Wilcox has made Helen less sure of her opinions. A third letter briefly reports that Helen has fallen in love with the younger son whom she has only just met.

Commentary

The novel opens with charming informality: the tone of its first sentence suggests that the narrator treats both his subject and his audience with a touch of wry detachment. Helen's letter begins with the character and setting of Howards End which are to acquire such significance during the course of the novel. It introduces the central question of the book: what are Schlegels to think of Wilcoxes? The first chapter tells through Helen's letters the story of a complete episode which is to the novel as a whole as an embryo to a mature adult. It opens with Helen's reversal of assumptions the sisters made when they first met the Wilcoxes. It develops with Helen's apparent intellectual defeat as she submits to the stronger opinions of Mr Wilcox and ends with her falling in love with the younger son of the family.

Helen is a woman with 'advanced' opinions for 1910. She has strong and clear opinions of her own, but she is obviously impulsive and enjoys being swept off her feet. She also seems to enjoy entering imaginatively into the lives of others. But there are traces in her letters of contradictions which will be developed later in the novel. Compared with her own brother, the Wilcox men are admirably strong; but they suffer from hay-fever, unlike Mrs Wilcox who enjoys smelling hay. She enjoys the strength of the Wilcoxes, even when Mr Wilcox is knocking her opinions to pieces, but she refers to them as 'a clan', to the house, when they are all there, as 'a rabbit warren', and it may be wondered whether 'living like fighting cocks' is a complete recipe for a good life. And how comfortably do the traces of earlier ways of life – 'a tomb with trees in it, a hermit's house' – consort with the tennis, cricket and bridge of comfortable, middle-class Edwardian England?

CHAPTER 2

Summary
Margaret Schlegel receives the news of Helen's love affair as she breakfasts in London with her aunt. She explains they met the Wilcoxes when they were on holiday in Germany, although she knows little about them. She loves her sister and wants to be with her but she cannot go because her brother is ill. Aunt Juley, who thinks to herself as a practical person, offers to go instead. Margaret urges her to speak only to Helen about the matter. She sees her off to the station and returns to find a telegram from Helen informing her that the affair is over.

Commentary
From now on the commentary of the narrator assumes a crucial significance. Forster's narrative technique combines dramatised conversations, whose meaning may not be immediately obvious, with a commentary which is subtly elusive. In the first conversation between Margaret and Aunt Juley we notice the disparity between the speakers. Margaret is reticent and sceptical; her aunt is determined and downright. She thinks she is practical and clear-headed. Her

clumsy remark about the Germans draws our attention to the fact that the Schlegels themselves are partly German. On this fact rests a key distinction between the Schlegel sisters and almost all the other characters in the book. (The only 'real' Germans in the novel are dull, self-centred ordinary mortals.) The distinction rests on a difference between Continental and English philosophy, the first having been speculative, imaginative, and comprehensive, seeking to give a complete account of the life of men and the world they live in; the second avoiding speculation and theory-building, content to be pragmatic. So Aunt Juley believes in plans and definite answers to specific questions, Margaret relies on feelings of affection and on the sense of loyalty she has to her sister. (She nearly breaches this trust by showing her aunt Helen's previous letters, but stops in time, claiming she does not have them.)

One key metaphor and one of Forster's repeated abstract words appear in this chapter. The first is the metaphor of the sea. The Schlegels' house in Wickham Square is protected from the noise of London by a block of flats which Forster calls 'a promontory', protecting the old houses from the tide of London life. It is a settled family house under threat from the restless activity of modern civilisation. Another striking metaphor is applied to King's Cross Station which reminds Margaret of Infinity. The station appears the gateway to 'some eternal adventure'. But the metaphor is expressed in paradoxical terms. The station which represents infinity is represented by two arches 'colourless, indifferent' which support 'an unlovely clock'. The index of the timeless itself measures time. Forster's narrator hastily interposes to prevent the reader from thinking Margaret ridiculous, but the notion of there being points of time which may intersect with eternity is one which we will be asked to consider seriously as the action of the novel unfolds.

CHAPTER 3

Summary
The Schlegel sisters were left orphans when their brother Tibby (Theobald) was born. Mrs Munt, their aunt, had offered to look after them but their father had refused. He was German and Mrs Munt was suspicious of foreigners. She believes the sisters are in danger of throwing themselves away; they mix with people of 'advanced' views; they are cultured. Mrs Munt is cultured herself, but she believes in common sense. She travels to Howards End which is situated north of London and reached by train from a village made prosperous by commuters. There by chance she meets a member of the family whom she takes for Helen's fiancé. They talk at cross-purposes on the

way to Howards End. When Charles Wilcox discovers the mistake, a heated dispute ensues. He thinks Helen is as unsuitable for his brother, Paul, as Mrs Munt thinks Paul unsuitable for Helen. When they arrive at Howards Ends, Helen runs out to say the affair is over. But Charles has summoned Paul to ask whether the news is true and Mrs Wilcox is obliged to intervene, bringing a public scene to a civilised end. She tells Charles that 'they do not love any longer'.

Commentary
This chapter is an excellent example of Forster's control of a kind of comedy which borders on farce but whose undertones have darker implications. Forster quickly establishes the differences between the Schlegels and Mrs Munt by distinguishing their easy self-possession from her provincial narrow-mindedness. Forster's description of her journey to Howards End further develops the theme of the contrast between the old and the new features of the landscape. The age of the railway and motor car has preferred convenience and speed to closer contact with the natural environment: the ancient tombs of Danish soldiers are almost swamped by modern bungalows.

Forster handles the comedy of the misunderstanding between Charles and Mrs Munt with vivacity. His perfunctory politeness and off-hand slang ('Wait a mo . . . our motor's here. I'll run you up in it') is cleverly contrasted with her lumbering tact. Mrs Munt's pleasure in the comfort of the car and the wealth its possession implies is contrasted with his unawareness of her own sense of status. Charles is noticeably rude to inferiors; Mrs Munt breaks her promise to Margaret not to speak to anyone but Helen. These discordant ingredients produce loud voices and an open quarrel. The scene is ended by Mrs Wilcox, a natural aristocrat who worships the past. The wisp of hay she carries in her hand has now become a sign of her link with the countryside. Her curiously flat reference to Helen and Paul's love suggests a certain remoteness from the emotions of ordinary folk. As she turns to smell a rose, it may seem that she disclaims them.

CHAPTER 4

Summary
Helen returns to London with her aunt. She had been fascinated by the power of the Wilcoxes to subvert her liberal prejudices. When Paul arrived, she had fallen in love with him and he had responded to her interest. But next day the confidence of the Wilcoxes seemed less assured: Helen had wondered if anything lay behind their prosperous façade. The Schlegel sisters reflect on the world of business which

seems so remote from their own. The Wilcox world of practical efficiency fails to deal with personal relationships, so prized by the Schlegels.

The sisters resume their life of cultural and intellectual pursuits. Their father had been a German who had fought for his country. But he belonged in spirit to a Germany which placed culture before conquest. He had abandoned a Germany which pursued commercial success, and he had come to believe that Europe no longer valued the imaginative powers which had nurtured its spirit; money and territorial expansion were now considered more important. Caught between German and British imperialism, the Schlegels are critical of both sides. Margaret had grown up believing in the supreme value of the individual: Helen agreed with her but she is more attractive than Margaret and more likely to be attracted, and influenced, by others.

Commentary

In this chapter Forster stops to explain the background of the situation he has plunged into, making a point of enlarging upon the tradition of German idealism on which the Schlegels draw. Forster introduces phrases which will resonate through the novel. An example is the 'collision' which has brought Helen and Paul together. Helen will come to forget that she has known Paul and yet the memory of her feeling for him will remain as a standard by which later feelings will be judged. Here is another example of the point of intersection between the temporary and accidental and what is permanent and enduring. Another key phrase which resounds through the novel is 'panic and emptiness', referring to Helen's sense of the confused impotence which is hidden by the Wilcox family's confident façade. They may appear to have 'their hands on all the ropes' but the business world is one of 'telegrams and anger' – modern speed and convenience linked to explosive negative feeling. Helen no longer doubts her own belief in the inner life of sympathetic imagination and loyalty between friends. But Forster's account of the sisters suggests that there is a difference between them. Helen is more liable to be swayed by emotion; Margaret is more clear-sighted and more direct. She is ready to accept that putting the Schlegel principles into practice may occasionally fail.

CHAPTER 5

Summary

At a concert, the Schlegels, their aunt and some German friends, listen to Beethoven's Fifth Symphony. They respond to the music in characteristically individual ways. Helen thinks of goblins walking over the universe and of the 'panic and emptiness' she discovered in the Wilcoxes. The music seems to say that there is an aspect of the world which defeats human optimism and effort.

Helen leaves the concert hall, taking by mistake the umbrella of a young man to whom Margaret has been talking. He appears to think he has been robbed. Margaret invites him back to retrieve the umbrella. He is interested in music and literature but is not of Margaret's class. He admires Margaret's range of interest, but he is preoccupied with his umbrella. It is found at Wickham Place but Helen's reference to its dilapidated state upsets its owner, who hurries off. The sisters agree that it is worth trusting strangers, even if a price has occasionally to be paid for it, though Margaret thinks some prices may be too high. The incident reminds them of the gulf between the comfortable middle classes and those whose lives are deformed by poverty.

Commentary
The apparently trivial nature of the events in this chapter should not blind the reader to its real significance. Its opening sentence challenges and teases the reader: are we bound to accept its blandly authoritative statements? Forster uses the symphony to differentiate his characters: it is easy to see that the German cousin and her young man are not very intelligent, that Mrs Munt is conventional, Tibby academic. Margaret appears to be displaying the right attitude in listening only to the music, but Helen's rather fanciful account of it may have support from the narrator. It is not easy to be sure, for the narrative voice becomes intertwined here with Helen's thoughts. At the paragraph which begins, 'For the Andante had begun', the phrase 'to Helen's mind' suggests that most of what follows is what she thinks. Helen wants her companions to listen for the return of the goblins who seem to suggest that life is worthless. The repeated phrase, 'Panic and emptiness! Panic and emptiness!' reflects her vision of what life might mean. But at the end of a subsequent paragraph it is not entirely clear whether the sentences, 'But the goblins were there. They could return. He had said so bravely, and that is why one can trust Beethoven when he says other things' are further extensions of Helen's thought or whether these opinions are now supported by the narrator. The point is worth thinking about: these early chapters tend to contrast Helen unfavourably with Margaret. But perhaps there are times when her judgement, however apparently irrational, is right.

Forster establishes the type of the as yet unnamed young man with a rapidity which has seemed unconvincing to some readers. For them this character is a caricature. Perhaps Forster drew on his own teaching experience here. He presents a man who aspires to art and 'culture' but is held back by many social disadvantages. He worries about how much he is spending; he has learned not to trust other people; 'most of his energies went on defending himself from the unknown!' The young man provides a test for the Schlegels' social theory: better to trust, they believe, even if the trust is sometimes misplaced.

Where Margaret and Helen are anxiously ethical, their brother Tibby is concerned only with the satisfaction of his own pleasures, though they are fastidiously well-chosen. He perhaps represents the effeminacy which the Schlegel virtues could lead to, if pursued to excess. The Wilcox virtues are seen as masculine; pursued excessively, they might produce brutality. At their best the Schlegels are an oasis of liberal virtue, constantly threatened by a hostile world on which they depend, since their leisure is financed by investments which take a share of the profits of work done by other people.

CHAPTER 6

Summary
The young man's name is Leonard Bast. He lives on the edge of gentility but wants to prove his worth. He feels hurt by his encounter with the Schlegels. He lives in the basement of a London flat with a young woman called Jacky. The flat is new, garish, vulgar and temporary. As he enters he cuts his finger on the broken glass of a photograph of Jacky. He sits down to read a piece from John Ruskin's *Stones of Venice* , which he believes to be a masterpiece of English prose. Its loftiness seems out of place in his flat, but Leonard keeps hoping that his pursuit of culture will lead him to wealth. He is interrupted by Jacky, who does not share his interests. She is preoccupied with the subject of marriage. He tells her he will stand by her; they have a meal of processed food. Leonard plays the piano; Jacky goes to bed. Leonard fears he will never be able to match the ease and freedom of the Schlegels. Jacky urges him to come to bed, but he continues to read Ruskin whose words suggest that Nature has little interest in people like Leonard.

Commentary
Beware of mistaking Forster's tone. The flat assertiveness of the opening paragraph is a challenge to the reader as much as a confession of the author's own limitations. Novels – for Forster at least – deal with the middle ground of society. In the abyss of poverty, life is lived at too minimal a level to be comprehended by the imagination of the middle-class novelist. Forster's irony plays on the word 'Democracy', suggesting that equality is limited by considerations of money: those who do not meet certain financial standards do not qualify for inclusion in the kingdom of equals.

Once again, Forster describes London as a place of continual change: it has 'the restlessness of the water in a fountain'. Leonard lives in a flat which is likely to have a brief existence. It is part of the uneasy drift of change, brought about by the rising population whose possible levelling-off Mr Cunningham is ironically allowed to deplore. The theme of wealth and its connection with the leisured pursuits of civilised pleasure is taken up in the references to Ruskin's *Stones of Venice*. Here, John Ruskin (1819–1900) stands for a kind of civilisation out of Leonard's reach. For Leonard, the activities he associates with 'culture' are not ends in themselves, they are means of attaining wealth and leisure. He sees the Schlegels, as the Schlegels see the Wilcoxes: 'their hands were upon the ropes, once and for all'.

Leonard's flat, its furniture and the woman he lives with are far removed from the images presented to him by the books he reads. The flat is 'an amorous and not unpleasant little hole': whatever positive connotations are attached to the word 'amorous', they are subverted by that double negative and the derisive 'little hole'. Forster's description of Jacky is cruel – almost Swiftian in its detached description of physical particulars. She is presented as a living support for a grotesque collection of incongruous clothes, her face a spoiled image of her smashed photograph. Yet despite her vulgar self-assertiveness, she has 'anxious eyes'. Leonard hopes someday to 'push his head out of the grey waters and see the universe', but elsewhere he acknowledges that 'to see life steadily and to see it whole was not for the likes of him'. The narrator's account of the disparity between Ruskin in his gondola and Leonard in his basement should be read with care: 'the folly' and 'the misery' of such as Leonard are phrases that Forster attributes to Ruskin. The irony may be directed against the rich lover of art who may not have understood the message of the 'whispering lagoons'.

CHAPTER 7

Summary
Next day, Mrs Munt tells Margaret that the Wilcoxes have taken a flat opposite Wickham Place. She fears that Helen will be involved with them again. Margaret tells her aunt that Helen's feelings are altered, but Helen blushes when she hears the news. Margaret does not share her aunt's caution: she believes it is worth taking risks with human relationships, though she agrees that taking risks is easier for those who have money. Perhaps 'the very soul of the world' is economic. Differences in income may support different moral values. Later Helen tells Margaret that she intends to go to Germany. She will not in future fall in love with one of the Wilcoxes.

Commentary

This chapter is an excellent example of Forster's ability to maintain conventional narrative interest and to develop themes that interest him more deeply. Mrs Munt's anxiety about the state of Helen's emotions is a consequence of her idle – but human – curiosity about her surroundings, but her fussiness lacks insight. Helen appears to know more than she pretends about their neighbours. Margaret remembers Mr Wilcox well enough to praise his complexion. Her capacity for admiration – and Helen's for concealment – are pointers towards later developments.

In this chapter Helen decisively dissociates herself from the Wilcoxes, but Margaret begins her serious involvement with them. Forster's metaphors about the tides of change in London help us to see the city as akin to sea-girt Venice, whose rich art rested on commercial achievement. Margaret applies the same metaphor to her family. Their incomes are the foundation of a civilised life and they are constantly renewed from the labour of those who live in the abyss. Margaret is on the side of money, though she takes no sides about who should have it.

In contrast – and perhaps in contradiction – is her belief in the value of 'joy' – a spontaneous pleasure in life, which is not to be obtained by taking thought. If there is a contradiction in her position, Forster does not bring it to our attention. 'Money' and 'Joy' – like 'Joy' and 'Death' – are two of the abstract concepts whose conflict is recorded in the events which form the substance of this narrative.

CHAPTER 8

Summary

Mrs Wilcox, who had felt some affinity with Margaret when they met in Germany, calls on the Schlegels soon after her arrival in London. Margaret first writes to suggest they should not meet. When she learns that Paul has gone abroad, she goes round to apologise for her rudeness. Mrs Wilcox is in bed. She is glad that Paul and Helen will not meet: she had thought their passing affection unwise. Mrs Wilcox is bored by London: they had taken the flat to arrange Charles's wedding. Only the mention of Howards End interests her. She had been born there; it has almost magical associations for her. Underneath their conversation runs a more serious note: Mrs Wilcox wonders if Margaret has forgotten that she is a girl. Margaret assumes she is referring to her inexperience, though she is probably referring to her unused capacity for living. Margaret lists some of the virtues she tries to practise, though she admits they sometimes conflict and have to be brought into harmony. Mrs Wilcox appears to agree.

Commentary

The opening of this chapter is high-spirited burlesque, but the point about the wariness between the sexes, exemplified by Helen's reserved attitude to Tibby, is a serious one. The ideal of personal relationships may fail, it is surely hinted, at the barrier of sex. Margaret's treatment of Mrs Wilcox suggests some breach in her fidelity to the idea of friendship, though the relationship between the women is slight. Her visit to Mrs Wilcox in hat and shawl 'just like a poor woman' might be a tiny hint that Margaret's comments on money in the previous chapter are not Forster's final word.

The central event of this chapter is the interview between Margaret and Mrs Wilcox. It takes place in shifting lights which 'combined to create a strange atmosphere of dissolution'. Forster creates a clear distinction between Mrs Wilcox's indefiniteness and Margaret's stout common sense. Her opposition to Paul's love for Helen is based on instinct. She becomes uneasy when asked to be definite. The pause that precedes her 'I almost think you forget you're a girl' is described as a 'flicker', a 'quiver', a 'blur'; it is 'a pause of shifting and eternal shadows'. It may appear that Forster is simply hinting at Mrs Wilcox's approaching death, but the words lend an almost oracular weight to what follows. And the word 'blur' is the first in a series of Forster's uses of this word which eventually tells us much about Mrs Wilcox's attitude to the world. Margaret believes she is referring to her inexperience of life and produces a list of the virtues she tries to practise. But Mrs Wilcox's comment on what she says is ambiguous. When she says she would like to have spoken in the same way, does she mean that she regrets she is not as articulate as Margaret, or does she find Margaret's directness simple-minded? Or is she thinking of an experience which she has had but which Margaret is not in a position to understand? What that experience might be is surely connected to Howards End, the only topic which arouses Mrs Wilcox's interest. The mystery that surrounds Mrs Wilcox is given specific form when she remembers the wych-elm stuck with pigs' teeth at Howards End. When it is mentioned, there is an evident clash between her will to believe and Margaret's rationalism. At the end of the chapter Forster tells us that Mrs Wilcox's hand which earlier was surrounded by 'a quivery halo of light' is now withdrawn into 'the deeper shadows'. Is this another hint of her approaching death or does it suggest a more general scepticism about Margaret's common sense?

Notice how Forster repeats the little motif of the smashed photograph and the bleeding finger to suggest an incompatibility between
the characters concerned – this time, between Margaret and Dolly.
Does it also suggest an affinity between Margaret and Leonard?

CHAPTER 9

Summary
Margaret's luncheon party for Mrs Wilcox is not a success. The other
guests chatter about 'the politico-economical-aesthetic' topics which
the Schlegels enjoy discussing. Margaret praises the Germans
because they are 'on the look-out for beauty' and admire poetry. Mrs
Wilcox is silent. Margaret praises the English respect for freedom of
action but prefers European liberty of thought. Mrs Wilcox says they
never discuss anything at Howards End. She even suggests that action
and discussion might best be left to men. As she prepares to leave,
Mrs Wilcox comments on Margaret's 'interesting life'. Margaret has a
sudden feeling of revulsion against the superficiality of her existence.
According to Mrs Wilcox, old and young are 'all in the same boat'.
But Margaret's friends think she is dull.

Commentary
The free-wheeling conversation of this chapter repeats the contrast
between Germany and England. England values freedom of action – what Matthew Arnold called 'doing as one likes'; Germany
values 'the free play mind'. Mrs Wilcox appears to suggest a third set of
values, located for her in Howards End, rural rather than urban,
instinctive and non-discursive. Margaret and her friends represent a
superficial and rather unattractive intellectualism. When Mrs Wilcox
says that, whether people are old or young, interested in Art and
Literature or Politics and Sport, they are 'all in the same boat', she
uses a metaphor which will not be fully explicit until Chapter 11.
Notice that Margaret's conversation is 'the social counter-part of a
motor-car'; Mrs Wilcox's is 'a wisp of hay, a flower'. Forster's
metaphors are now sufficiently established for us to have no doubt
where his sympathies lie. When Mrs Wilcox is present 'the outline of
known things grew dim'. 'She and daily life were out of focus: one or
the other must show blurred'. To what significance does this simple
inarticulate woman point?

CHAPTER 10

Summary
Mrs Wilcox suggests to Margaret that they go Christmas shopping together. Margaret recommends making a list. Mrs Wilcox suggests that Margaret's name will be first on her list, but Margaret is interested in people, not things. Mrs Wilcox hopes she will think of a suitable gift. Margaret reflects on the incongruity of Christmas when religious ideals are expressed in the most materialistic way. Only private life, she believes, can adequately reflect spiritual values. Only personal relationships can represent the traditional idea of God. Mrs Wilcox discovers that Margaret expects to leave Wickham Place because it is to be pulled down to make way for new flats. She is horrified at the idea of Margaret losing the only home she has known. On impulse she invites her to visit Howards End. Margaret demurs and Mrs Wilcox seems annoyed. They go home through darkening London streets. Margaret feels she has been mistaken to refuse a spontaneous gesture of friendship. She goes to Mrs Wilcox's flat to find that she has gone away. She finds her at King's Cross Station. They are on the point of boarding the train when Mr Wilcox and his daughter arrive on the platform. The trip to Howards End is put off till another day.

Commentary
Chapter 10 continues the contrast between Margaret's business-like directness and Mrs Wilcox's indecision. Mrs Wilcox's wish to give Margaret a present points to later developments in the novel, but 'giving' here is associated with the vulgarity of modern Christmas. For Margaret, God is a metaphor for the sacred bond of personal relationship. Mrs Wilcox is more concerned with place: she is distressed that the Schlegels are to lose their home. Her invitation to Margaret to visit Howards End is a spontaneous gesture of trust (like Margaret's trusting Leonard Bast) but it is refused. Forster describes the city through which they return as 'Satanic'. The fog which lies upon it does no harm to trade, but it depresses the spirit. Mrs Wilcox, 'this shadowy woman', returns to her hotel, enters the cage of the lift and goes heavenward, 'like a specimen in a bottle', and the heaven to which she ascends is as black and sooty as hell.

Margaret has acted against her own ideals and in the darkness that descends she glimpses 'the invisible'. She sees the value Howards End has for Mrs Wilcox. The whimsical puzzle about King's Cross Station is now solved: the Infinity to which it leads is a kingdom of values, one of the components of which is friendship, another the sense of place. But Margaret is not to reach it in Mrs Wilcox's company.

CHAPTER 11

Summary
Mrs Wilcox has died and she is mourned by her neighbours in the country. Mr Wilcox remembers his wife's constancy, simplicity and good-will. The family attempt breakfast, remembering her. They expect life to resume its current, but there is an awkward surprise. A letter from the nursing home encloses a note asking her husband to give Howards End to Margaret. The family are surprised and angry. Not understanding what lies behind the request, they decide it would be wrong to obey her wish. They do, however, neglect a personal appeal. They wonder whether Margaret has had improper influence on her, or whether she knows of her intention. Mrs Wilcox's action appear a betrayal. Mr Wilcox attempts to defend Margaret: she had attended the funeral and sent ill-chosen flowers. In the end the family agree that the matter is best forgotten.

Commentary
Despite Forster's hints, Mrs Wilcox's death is abrupt and shocking. Only the young woodcutter, pollarding the elms, challenges death with his absorption in the joy of love. When he leaves the graveyard, there is a silent emptiness which Forster dwells on. He compares the church to a ship steering its company towards Infinity: perhaps this is the boat which (in Chapter 9) Mrs Wilcox said everybody was in. Love and Death appear irreconcilable opposites; the Infinity, in which they might be reconciled, impossible to imagine.

The everyday reality of the Wilcox family life has a less impressive ring. Forster expands the negative account the Schlegels have given of them. Father and son are described as obstinate. The elaborate 'fortress' metaphor developed for Mr Wilcox will remain part of his description until the last chapters of the novel. They place no value on personal relationships. Their conventional grief for Mrs Wilcox easily switches to astonishment and anger, when her posthumous note reaches them. Mrs Wilcox's wish is lost in legal considerations. Forster makes much of the Wilcox's masculinity: they are surly with servants and domineering to their womenfolk. To them, the emotions are like the songs the sirens sang to Ulysses – dangerous distractions from the business of life. (Notice that Margaret's chrysanthemums, which the Wilcoxes think unsuitable, are taken by the woodcutter as an emblem of love.)

CHAPTER 12

Summary
Mrs Wilcox's death has a deep effect on Margaret, who has heard

nothing of her intentions towards her. She is impressed by her dignity in the face of death. Mrs Wilcox seemed to suggest a standard of behaviour which might encourage hope for improved human relationships. Although Margaret had met the Wilcoxes by chance, she admires qualities which are very different from those of her own family. They can deal with the outer world. Margaret believes there may be merit in reconciling these practical virtues with the qualities of sensitivity which the Schlegels possess. Helen, meanwhile, has gone for a carefree holiday in Germany; Tibby is preparing for Oxford. Margaret receives a letter from Charles Wilcox, asking her if his mother wanted her to have anything. Mr Wilcox sends her a little decorative bottle which had belonged to his wife. Margaret decides she likes Mr Wilcox. Who could have predicted that things would turn out as they had done? She reflects on the unpredictability of life and on the danger of being too well-prepared for what may never happen. She resolves to remain open to the unexpected.

Commentary

The great commonplace image of life as a journey through mysterious and threatening seas to an unknown destination is elaborately employed in the opening paragraphs of this chapter. The grave stoicism of its account of Mrs Wilcox's demeanour as she faced death contains a hint that there may be qualities of the human spirit which death does not destroy. The 'fragments torn from the unknown' which are the true legacy she has left Margaret are elliptically suggested. For Margaret, 'truer relationships gleamed' – there might be 'hope even on this side of the grave' – but the reader must be prepared to suspend judgement and wait until events give substance to her intuitions. For the moment Margaret's hopes are attached to the Wilcox men. They are competent where the Schlegels are not; perhaps they have qualities she lacks. It is worth noticing how Margaret passes from an admiration for the dignity and sense of proportion of Mrs Wilcox to an admiration of the 'grit' and competence of the Wilcox men. The association is understandable, but is the reader convinced that the qualities displayed by Mrs Wilcox and her menfolk are consistent and compatible with one another? Margaret believes that they are and means to reconcile them further to her own. This chapter, which marks the end of the first phase of the novel, prepares for the second, which is Forster's account of the success of her attempt at reconcilement.

Now, Forster detaches Margaret from Tibby and Helen. He sends Tibby to Oxford where he learns to love things rather than people. There, we are told,

He made no friends. His Oxford remained Oxford empty, and he took into life with him, not the memory of a radiance, but the memory of a colour scheme.

It is a damning comment on the preference for aesthetic perfection over human warmth.

The account of Helen is more ambiguous. We see her through Margaret's eyes as someone to whom the lives of others have become less meaningful. Self-absorbed, she has forgotten the Wilcoxes. But Helen's 'decent pause' after Margaret has spoken well of Mrs Wilcox may not necessarily mean that she has lost interest in these matters. Nor is Margaret's conclusion that life is 'a romance' necessarily the one we must accept. If 'actual life is full of false clues and signposts that lead nowhere', what is the value of the insights she has gained from Mrs Wilcox's life and death? Or is Forster's narrator drawing attention to the difference between history and fiction?

CHAPTER 13

Summary
Two years pass. The Schlegels continue with their comfortable lives. The lease of their house expires and they must look for a new one. Tibby begins to think of what he will do when he leaves Oxford: he does not want to follow a profession or be troubled by a sense of duty. Helen bursts in to say that a rather vulgar woman has called to enquire for her husband. She thinks the episode is a joke; Margaret wonders if it is not a warning from a world they normally ignore.

Commentary
In the first sentence of this chapter Forster once more compares civilised life to an island in a shifting sea: London itself is 'a tract of quivering grey, intelligent without purpose, and excitable without love'. We notice the perfectly unobtrusive repetition of the word 'grey', which Forster uses so often to describe a life which is drab and meaningless. London is seen as a monstrous form of inhuman life, reactive but pointless. The notion that only a god made in our image could justify its existence is frightening rather than reassuring, since we can guess at the meanness of such a deity. Forster's irony is at its sharpest here as he appears to depreciate things he values – the love of earth, for example – and to praise an anthropomorphic religion which he could scarcely admire.

Margaret notices, but falls short of condemning, the reduced quality of life the city offers its citizens. Tibby has already decided to withdraw. Tibby chooses as a model for his own life the ineffectual Mr Vyse, who is a character in *A Room with a View*, but Margaret commends to his attention Mr Pembroke, a dully conventional character from *The Longest Journey*, linking his name with the Wilcoxes. Margaret's conversation with her brother – apparently trivial – is worth careful study since it suggests the complexities of her position. She admires work and duty – those grand Victorian virtues – but finds that they lead to London and to Empire, neither satisfactory.

The chapter ends in burlesque as Helen describes the visit of 'Mrs Lanoline' who 'asked for a husband as if he was an umbrella'. Margaret looking out at the flats opposite which 'hung like an ornate curtain between [her] and the welter of London', has a premonition of tragedy and a glimpse of how near the Schlegels might be to the chaotic meaninglessness that London represents. (At the beginning of the chapter we are told that the city is 'emblematic of their lives'.) What are they to do when their remnant of an older London is itself swept away in the tide of change?

CHAPTER 14

Summary

Next day Leonard Bast arrives to remind the Schlegels that they had met him at a concert and had given him their card. His wife had found it after Leonard had disappeared the previous Saturday. He explains that he had wanted to get in touch with nature and had walked into the country. When he failed to return that night, his wife had thought he might be with them. He had not had the adventure he had hoped for: in the country he was tired, hungry and cold. But he had tried to escape from routine to a life of reality. Although he owes his interest in the countryside to the books he has read, he managed to find at first-hand the experience the books referred to. The sisters invite him to come back again, but he says he does not want to spoil the memory of the talk he has had with them. Leonard's meeting with the Schlegels brings him into contact with the life of 'culture'. Hitherto he had believed education to be a means to social advancement. Now he believes that literature may point to ways of living which are valuable in themselves. As he walks along Regent Street, people look at him with hostility. He realises he is not wearing his hat: as soon as he puts it on, and looks like everyone else, the hostility ceases.

Commentary

In this chapter Forster 'places' Leonard Bast. He is an 'accusing presence' haunting the city which has deprived him of his birthright as a countryman, though it has not quite destroyed his good looks or his physical robustness. It has given him, as a poor substitute, a pale reflection of what he has lost in the fashionable books about country life he has thought it would be 'cultured' to read. The chapter resounds with the names of writers who at the end of the nineteenth century had celebrated the 'artistic cult' of the Earth which Forster in the previous chapter says 'has had its day'. Reading their works has been the stimulus to Leonard's adventure, but instead of Romance he has found fact. Forster compares fact to 'a pebble', as if Leonard had rediscovered a link with his pastoral ancestor, and was a David using pebble and sling against the Goliath of a false modern culture which prefers words to things. The sisters – Helen in particular – are excited by his enterprise in breaking with routine, but at the end of the chapter, it looks as if Leonard has returned to the comfort of ordinary life. He has reverted to being a citizen of London. The artificial skies created above the city by its own illumination suit his preference for keeping romance apart from reality. His walk into the country may have pierced the skin of unreality which darkens his imagination, but it has not wholly broken it. For the reader, however, Leonard's adventure may be the first major clue to the nature and source of Margaret's – and Forster's – 'hope this side of the grave'.

CHAPTER 15

Summary
The topic at the evening party which the sisters attend that night is how a millionaire ought to leave his money for the benefit of society. Leonard Bast's name is used as a synonym for the deserving poor. How is his condition to be improved without spoiling his independence? Margaret believes that men like him should simply be given money: by using money they will become civilised. As the sisters walk home they decide not to keep up with Mr Bast: they must not play at friendship. They talk about Margaret's views on money: if it is the foundation of life, what will be its superstructure? According to Margaret, whatever the individual decides. For her, places may become more important than people. She mentions Mrs Wilcox; by chance Mr Wilcox is sitting nearby. They tell him about their discussion and about Leonard Bast. He advises them that Leonard should leave his present job because his company is in a bad state. He tells Margaret that Howards End has been let. The sisters tell him they are about to move, too. After they separate, the sisters agree to warn Leonard about his company's affairs.

Commentary
Margaret's thoughts on money are here given their most organised form. Money is essential to a civilised life, because it is the means of realising the aspirations of the individual. What these aspirations are may be left to the individual: Oxford, walking at night, Wickham Place, Howards End are all rational objects of desire, and there

seems no reason to prefer one to the other. Are we to believe that this easy relativism about ideals is Forster's last word? For the first time, Margaret unconsciously echoes a theme which originated with Mrs Wilcox — the importance of place.

When the sisters meet Mr Wilcox on the Embankment, Forster is careful to make distinctions. Where the Schlegels find mystery in the Thames, Mr Wilcox sees it as a business proposition. Where Helen bridles at his patronising tone, Margaret is submissive – perhaps, like Evie, she should be breeding dogs instead of debating – and quite ready to admire his 'high forehead confronting the stars'. She is completely unaware that the high forehead serves as a fortress. About Howards End Mr Wilcox is indifferent. His description of it and of the old woman who lives nearby – and whom we shall shortly meet – is demeaning. His exclamation, 'Full tide', as he looks over the parapet into the river, may be an expression of satisfaction at the amplitude of his own fortune, but Margaret, seeing it on the ebb can only see it as an emblem of the fickleness of human affection. It is as if the restless change which is a feature of the external world has begun to affect the human spirit itself.

CHAPTER 16

Summary
Leonard comes to tea but the visit is a failure. The Schlegels want to talk about Leonard's job, but he regards this as an intrusion. His hour of romance with educated women is dissipated in talk about money and interrupted by the arrival of Evie and Mr Wilcox. When the Schlegels ask Leonard to come again, he refuses and Helen complains of his rudeness. He accuses them of patronising him and of attempting to find out about his employer. They remind him of his walk in the country, of their desire to help him because they thought he shared their wish to struggle against dullness and narrowness. When Leonard goes, pursued by Helen, the Wilcoxes praise Margaret for putting him in his place. Mr Wilcox suggests that Leonard is not a type they should know. Margaret insists that she has wanted to help Leonard get in touch with reality through friendship or the love of place. Mr Wilcox says that Leonard is probably happy with his own life. Margaret tells the Wilcoxes Leonard's story, but they prefer to think he spent his weekend with another woman. Margaret defends Leonard and suddenly sees that Mr Wilcox is jealous. Helen has seen Leonard out and realises now that he was upset because he wanted to talk about literature. As they leave the Schlegels, Mr Wilcox says they should have someone to look after them.

Commentary

The opening dialogue between Leonard and the Schlegels is written in the style of demure social comedy. The tensions of Leonard's divided life are comically, but not unsympathetically, revealed as his attempts to pursue cultured conversation are undermined by the Schlegels' practicality. Even his conception of the company for which he works is romanticised. He is willing to believe in the composite image created by the advertiser which links insurance to Church and State and invests it with all the associations of classical antiquity. That Porphyrion was a legendary giant who rebelled against the gods is a joke that Forster does not stop to explain. Leonard is not intelligent enough to understand the intentions of Margaret and Helen. His attempts at culture seem to them clumsy and old-fashioned – he likes the works of Thomas Carlyle (1795–1881) whose reputation remained powerful among self-educated working men long after it had faded elsewhere. The comic tone changes after the arrival of the Wilcoxes. Leonard becomes strident; the talk bursts into incandescence as Margaret reminds Leonard of the idealism of his adventure. Taking up his stuttered 'I — I', she tries to appeal to the pioneer in him and break down the barriers he has erected between what is real and what is romantic in his life. Forster is skilful in integrating key concepts of the novel into this superficially 'realistic' scene: Evie's uncomprehending laughter punctuates Margaret's attempts to help Leonard to share her view of him. Leonard himself fails to see the connection between his real and his ideal self. The question of Mr Wilcox's responsibility for Leonard – so crucial in later chapters – is raised for the first time. Margaret's attempt to show Leonard how to 'get upsides with life' reminds us that Leonard himself (in Chapter 14) had used this very phrase of 'culture'. She herself speaks of the necessity of 'some very dear person or some very dear place', seeing these as alternatives. In reply, Mr Wilcox defends London and the anger he confesses to feeling about her antipathy towards it makes some inroads in Margaret's position.

It is in this chapter that Forster first sounds the note of passion. Mr Wilcox is moved to jealousy by Margaret's interest in Leonard. For a moment his defences fall and Margaret sees 'the real man in him'. She sees his jealousy and the anger it has generated. She is able to control and modify the momentary self-satisfaction this gives her: she does not realise that behind his defences Mr Wilcox's feelings persist.

CHAPTER 17

Summary

It is time for the Schlegels to leave Wickham Place: Margaret begins to feel the strength of the affection she has for their belongings. But she has to find a new place to live. She is invited to have lunch with Evie and her fiancé. When she arrives at the restaurant, Mr Wilcox is there too. She tells him that she must find a new home but despairs of doing so. Inconsequential talk about the supernatural leads to Margaret asking about Howards End. Perhaps Mr Wilcox could let it to them. He tells her to be businesslike about moving house. They talk of Leonard and the class system. Margaret reflects on how quickly her acquaintance with Mr Wilcox has developed. She suspects the invitation to the restaurant was really his. Next day the Schlegels go off on their annual visit to Mrs Munt.

Commentary

To the accompaniment of the chatter of the newly-engaged Evie and Mr Cahill, Margaret and Henry Wilcox talk in a restaurant steeped in an atmosphere of Englishness which Forster clearly intends his readers to think artificial. Around them people talk about Empire, and the theme of Anglo-German rivalry is hinted at again. Forster makes it clear that he does not believe there is any real continuity between the England of Fielding and the England of Kipling, despite the contrary assumption of the ambience he has selected for this scene. Margaret's mood is depressed: she sees 'the vessel of life itself slipping past her'. The conversation between her and Mr Wilcox has little form. It moves inconsequentially from houses to food and back again and is perhaps only intelligble as a prelude to a proposal of marriage. Beneath the conversation, contrary sets of assumptions attempt some reconciliation. Whether in the choice of fish pie or mutton, Gruyere or Stilton, Margaret and Mr Wilcox seem scarcely compatible. Her interest in health food and theosophy are at odds with his stolidly conventional opinions. Her talk of houses being 'alive' seems unintelligible to him and reminds him of Leonard, whom he can only see as a member of a class, rather than the individual Margaret has seen. Margaret may be willing to be impressed by Mr Wilcox but Forster has made it clear to the reader how different they are in interests and attitudes. It is still an open question whether these differences matter.

CHAPTER 18

Summary

While visiting Mrs Munt at Swanage, Margaret receives a letter from Mr Wilcox offering to let to her his house in London. Margaret wonders if he is trying to get her to London for some purpose of his own – perhaps to propose – but she goes, feeling lonely and old-maidish. She finds that Mr Wilcox is lonely too, especially now that his daughter is to be married. Mr Wilcox appears as competent as ever, and she does not find him unattractive. They examine the house, which is substantial and masculine. In the drawing room Mr Wilcox asks her to become his wife. She is pleased and promises to give him an answer by letter. It is the first time Margaret has been proposed to by a man who interested her. She realises he has his limitations and decides to respect them. She thinks of Mrs Wilcox, and believes she would have approved.

Commentary
In this chapter the relationship between Margaret and Mr Wilcox advances to the threshold of marriage but Forster's account must be read with care. Margaret first thinks of marriage at Swanage as she sits 'gazing at mincing waves'. Views are as important in *Howards End* as they were in *A Room with a View*. It does not seem possible to neglect the associations Forster has created for 'tides' and 'waves'. The word 'mincing' has an impudent inappropriateness to Margaret's mood. Margaret's uncertainty is not helped by her family's response to Mr Wilcox's offer of a house. In London, she displays her sense of the value of the personal by calling Mr Wilcox's chauffeur by name and by remembering the name of his parlour maid. Margaret's mention of the servants is not taken up by Mr Wilcox; her reference to Parliament, which is surely positive, though brief, is responded to dismissively. For a moment Margaret is ashamed of her responsiveness:

> She could not concentrate on details. Parliament, the Thames, the irresponsive chauffeur, would flash into the field of house-hunting, and all demand some comment or response. It is impossible to see modern life steadily and see it whole, and she had chosen to see it whole. Mr Wilcox saw steadily. He never bothered with the mysterious or the private.

Despite this, Margaret 'liked being with him'. His eyes had 'an agreeable menace in them'.

It would surely be a mistake to believe that Forster means us to accept Margaret's judgement. We must remember that these paragraphs are records of Margaret's thoughts and not comments by the author. The 'free indirect speech' which Forster uses here may easily be mistaken for objective narration, and indeed the narrator may move imperceptibly from report to commentary. Margaret's meditation on Mr Wilcox ends as follows:

> Some day – in the millenium – there may be no need for his type. At present, homage is due to it from those who think themselves superior, and who possibly are.

It is of considerable significance for our understanding of the novel whether we read these sentences as Margaret's own view or as a judgement offered by the narrator.

The qualities Margaret admires in Mr Wilcox are exemplified by his house. She is equally prepared to admire its masculine virtues – its heaviness and over-decoration, its ostentatious suggestions of plunder. She is even ready to enjoy the comfort of chairs which look 'as if a motor-car has spawned'. But Forster's careful preparation has ensured that we know that motor-cars cannot be admired. He also makes it clear that none of the furniture in Ducie Street comes from Howards End.

When Mr Wilcox makes his proposal, we are told that an indescribable joy comes over her which proceeds from 'a central radiance' which she decides 'had been love'. But are we quite convinced? When we read that Margaret had kept the interview 'in tints of the quietest grey', we cannot forget the association Forster has established for this word. So, when 'waves of emotions' break over her 'as if a tide of passion was flowing through the night air', we cannot forget the destructive associations of 'tide'. Margaret decides to respect the defences Mr Wilcox has raised around his private life. He could not, except perhaps as a duty, talk of love, or 'open his heart'. She must neither expect nor demand anything of the kind from him. The sincerity of Margaret's feeling is obvious, but can we be sure her judgement is to be trusted?

CHAPTER 19

Summary

Frieda Mosebach, the Schlegels' German cousin, now married, is brought up to the hills outside Corfe, in Dorset, to see the countryside around the valley of the Stour. It is one of the finest parts of England, from which the imagination can move to Salisbury Plain and central England. The signs of the encroachment of London are visible, but the Isle of Wight is a symbol of the essential purity of England. As they admire the countryside, the Schlegels see the train bringing Margaret back from London. Tibby goes to meet Margaret; she shyly tells Helen that Mr Wilcox has proposed to her. Helen laughs at the idea, then, seeing Margaret is serious, bursts into tears. She warns Margaret not to marry him. Margaret explains how their relationship has developed, but she has to admit that it has not quite grown to love. Helen explains that her feelings against the Wilcoxes have to do with her own experience with Paul. Then she felt it was impossible to connect her concern for personal relationships with the business world. Margaret agrees that Mr Wilcox fears emotion and may not be as honest as herself, but she refuses to despise the

Wilcoxes. They have produced the conditions for civilisation in England; their work guarantees the income on which Margaret's life is based. Her love for Mr Wilcox may be prosaic but it is more soundly based than Helen's feelings for Paul. As night falls, the narrative returns to the seascape. Does England belong to those who have made her powerful or does it belong to those who have had the imagination to understand her true nature?

Commentary
This is a crucial chapter in the novel. It begins and ends with a vision of England, written in Forster's most impassioned prose. It is a complex chapter in which Reason is pitted against Imagination, industrial expansion against the traditional values of rural England. In this chapter Forster's imagination uses the landscape of England as a test of the values of those who create her destiny. The vision of England extends north to Salisbury Plain, where some of Forster's own most striking experiences of the English countryside had taken place, and east to London. There is no mistaking the dichotomy set up between the values these geographical locations imply. Northwards, the eye leads the imagination to the open country; eastwards, lie suburban houses and the commuter trail which leads to London. Swanage itself suggests the deterioration which Forster fears is threatening England. Southampton and Portsmouth, the first 'hostess to the nations', the second 'a latent fire' are ambiguously described. Around the coast 'with double and treble collision of tides, swirls the sea'. The collocation of 'collision' and 'tide' suggests the encroachment of chance and disorder which threatens the beauty of the country and puts in question the aims of its civilisation.

Reason cannot disentangle the forces which combine to create the present condition of England; only imagination can comprehend their complexity. Forster guides the responses of his readers by describing the responses of his characters to the landscape. Mrs Munt directs their attention to the swelling conurbations of Bournemouth, Swanage and Poole. Frieda contrasts them unfavourably with German rural scenes and the contrast between German and English sensibility is revived. When Frieda says, 'one is certain of nothing but the truth of one's emotions', Forster specifically gives the remark a German context, but it is difficult not be reminded of a famous passage from the letters of John Keats:

> I am certain of nothing but the holiness of the Heart's affections and the truth of Imagination – What the Imagination seizes as Beauty must be Truth – whether it existed before or not.

Beneath the desultory surface of the conversation lie issues which are central to the debate between Romanticism and Rationalism, between the pursuit of spiritual or material values.

Against this complex synthesis of landscape and allusion, Forster sets the subsequent discussion between Margaret and Helen. Helen's initial response to Margaret's news is purely emotional: she repeats her judgement of what the Wilcoxes stand for – 'Panic and emptiness' – stretches her hands 'towards the view' and bursts into tears. Margaret finds to her surprise that she has done the same. More rationally, Margaret recollects when she was first aware of Mr Wilcox's feelings for her, but in answer to a direct question whether she loves, him, she is obliged to say 'No'. Forster's treatment of Margaret at this point is complex. As she reviews the state of her feelings, the narrator says:

> It is pleasant to analyse feelings while they are still only feelings and unembodied in the social fabric. With her arm round Helen, and her eye shifting over the view, as if this county or that could reveal the secret of her own heart, she meditated honestly, and said, 'No'.

It is easy to detect the gentle irony implied by the word 'pleasant'. Forster underlines the gap that exists between feeling and action, between intention and the inevitable and unforeseen consequences of decisions, once they have been taken. And there does seem to be some link between 'the view' and Margaret's honest expression of her feelings. Does her honesty put in doubt the conclusion she had reached in the previous chapter about 'the central radiance' which she believed had pervaded Mr Wilcox's proposal to her?

Despite her clear-sighted acknowledgement of Mr Wilcox's deficiencies of character and imagination and even of honesty, Margaret defends her admiration of him. According to her, the Wilcox ethic of work has created the conditions which guarantee her life of intellect, imagination and human sympathy. As opposed to Helen's 'romance' with Paul, her own marriage will be 'well-considered prose'. The contrast seems plausible, but it would be rash to conclude that Margaret has won the debate. Margaret is securely on the side of reason and of 'thinking things out', but she may have neglected the claims of the unseen. Her affirmation of the value of the Wilcoxes to English civilisation is emphatic enough, but Helen's 'One would lose something' cannot be ignored. It seems to be supported by the darkness which spreads over the landscape and the shrinkage that its foreshortening seems to produce.

Forster's writing here produces a curious – and to some, uncomfortable – effect of dissonance: the tide advances over the shore; the landscape which had been laid out for our admiration becomes 'blackened' and 'sombre', yet the 'displacement' is 'a triumph', as if the virtues of the landscape have been concentrated rather than diminished. His final vision of England stresses its 'life' and 'joy', though the question of meaning and purpose is left open. Who can best lay claim to the spirit of England – Wilcoxes or Schlegels, men of action or men of imagination? Forster applies to the whole country the image of a ship of souls he first applied to the churchyard in which Mrs Wilcox was buried. England is seen, as Shakespeare saw it, 'lying as a jewel in a silver sea'. It is also a ship of destiny – the leading ship in a flotilla of nations. But who is in charge of it and to what eternal destiny is it bound? Forster leaves the question open, but calls in aid of answer 'the north wind' to oppose 'her rising seas'. If there is a contest between imagination and reason, between country and town, between Schlegels and Wilcoxes, there can be little doubt where his sympathies lie. But Margaret's aim is the reconciliation of opposites.

CHAPTER 20

Summary
The following day Henry Wilcox arrives with the engagement ring. As they walk that evening on the Parade, Margaret remembers their earlier meeting on Chelsea Embankment. She wants to talk about their relationship; he wants to talk business. She wants to know how he has got with her sister and brother. He wants to explain the financial arrangements he has made for his children. Margaret is frank about her income; Henry is more reticent. They discuss what is to be done about Henry's London house and when they are to be married. The last point raises ribald laughter from some passing youths which continues through the rest of their conversation. They agree to marry in September. Margaret would like to live in Howards End, but it has been let. Henry thinks they can have a house in the country and one in London, though Ducie Street now appears to have unsuspected drawbacks. Rather more protective than Margaret thinks necessary, Henry sees her home and clumsily tries to kiss her. The episode displeases her; it had not been prepared for and has not led to tenderness.

Commentary
When love is compared to a pebble – by Margaret or the narrator or both – the reader is reminded of the earlier use of the metaphor in Chapter 14. There, the pebble represents hard fact and sincerity. Here, it is a fact which will come to be recognised as one of the glories of human creativity. Love is a force that stands in opposition to both time and death, but it is not certain from the account given in this chapter whether Margaret has found the precious jewel of absolute love. In its public form, love is a business arrangement. As a husband, Henry would be little different from the man she had come to know. Besides, Margaret realises that a proposal of marriage is 'a suggestion, a seed' – the beginning, not the end, of a relationship.

The conversation between them at the beginning of this chapter is at cross-purposes: Margaret's concern for the personal is met by Henry's interest in business. When Margaret talks about money, she does so in a briskly rational fashion that Henry finds disconcerting. He is unwilling to be frank about money, just as he has failed to be frank about the faults of the flat in Ducie Street. The narrator suggests that there is 'a flaw inherent in the business mind' which 'Margaret may do well to be tender to' but the flaw, after all, is dishonesty. A curious passage between them may well imply a doubt about the soundness of Margaret's judgement. She tells Henry she mistrusts rivers and is about to say a word in favour of the sea, when she is interrupted by the mocking voices of the crude young men who act as chorus to their love-scene. Mr Wilcox's 'High tide' echoes a similar phrase he used at their meeting on the Embankment in Chapter 15. The associations which by now attach to 'rivers' and 'tides' may well suggest that Margaret is making a mistake.

Forster commends Margaret's insight into Henry's character: her power over him comes from her knowledge of him. But she still has to deal with what he does. When he kisses her awkwardly, it is clear that his concept of love has little in common with the 'jewel' celebrated at the beginning of the chapter. It is a clumsy manifestation of animal passion. For a moment, Margaret compares her relationship to Henry to that between Helen and Paul, but she does not draw Helen's conclusion (in Chapter 19) that it is therefore 'impossible'.

CHAPTER 21

Summary

Charles Wilcox, having heard of his father's intention to marry Margaret, blames his wife for helping to bring the relationship about. He believes that Margaret wants to get hold of Howards End.

Commentary

This chapter gives us a glimpse of the Wilcoxes at home. Charles is the most obviously unattractive member of the family. He is rude and overbearing to his wife. He can see only the worst in his father's engagement. He has no time for the 'artistic beastliness' of the Schlegels. Forster rounds off the chapter with a sketch of the scene: it is thoroughly suburban, presided over by Charles's motor-car. Children, just like Charles, are there, and more are expected. The Wilcoxes will 'inherit the earth' – a dismal prospect.

CHAPTER 22

Summary,
The events of the previous evening have not affected Margaret's love for Henry Wilcox. She hopes that she will be able to help him connect the world of passion with the world of prose, but Henry is not good at noticing things and believes in ignoring inessentials. They meet in the garden with Helen who has heard from Leonard Bast. On the sisters' advice he has left his position for a lower paid job with a safer firm. Mr Wilcox is impatient with talk about Leonard; he wants to talk about the tenancy of Howards End. He suggests they should go down there but Margaret does not want to offend her aunt by cutting short her visit. Margaret recalls some of the folklore attached to the wych-elm at Howards End but Mr. Wilcox has not heard of it. She tells Helen that Leonard Bast's new job is safe but Helen is not satisfied. She believes they have given wrong advice and should take responsibility. Mr Wilcox believes it is all part of the battle of life, which is at the mercy of impersonal forces which nevertheless tend towards progress. Margaret is afraid of a quarrel. She is glad to seize the opportunity of visiting Howards End.

Commentary
The first five paragraphs of the chapter are concerned with Margaret's hopes for the redemption of Henry Wilcox. The rainbow bridge which the narrator refers to is surely connected with the rainbow over which, in *Das Rheingold*, by Richard Wagner, the gods walked across the Rhine to Valhalla. In Forster's short story, 'The Celestial Omnibus' the rainbow bridge is the route which connects everyday life to the world of the imagination. Here it connects 'the prose in us with the passion'. When the connection is made, love is born; but Forster cannot claim that it is made in the soul of Henry Wilcox. His soul is 'a chaos'. He has been coerced by religious belief into believing that sex (or 'bodily passion', as Forster puts it) is bad. He does not believe this with the single-mindedness of a saint; his belief simply prevents him from being able to love his wife-to-be. Henry is unable to 'connect' because he does not notice the interests and feelings of other people. He has no imagination.

The conversation that follows illustrates his obtuseness. Margaret has done her best to link Henry and Helen by taking their hands that morning. She knows that Helen does not approve of her engagement, but she wants to bring Henry and her family together. Henry does not hear the dismay in Margaret's voice when he casually reveals that the insurance firm that Leonard Bast has left is quite safe. He is intent on his own business about Howards End. His only attempt at personal relations is to make small talk with Mrs Munt and Frieda. Helen detaches herself. Henry steers Margaret to the seaward side of the house. They look out at the bourgeois little bay, which must have yearned all through the centuries for just such a place as Swanage to be built on its margin. The waves were colourless, and the Bournemouth steamer, drawn up against the pier and hooting wildly for excursionists, gave a further touch of insipidity.

It is a depressing outlook: all the associations which the towns, the sea and the waves have gathered during the novel suggest the restrictions of the view. The bay is 'bourgeois' and has longed through centuries for its own destruction; the Bournemouth steamer is excited by the thought of the tourists who will destroy what they seek to admire. Margaret does not shirk discussing Leonard's problem with Henry: she is lucid, logical and exact about his predicament, but she readily accepts Henry's assurance that Leonard has not suffered from his change of employment. When he suggests going down to Howards End, she manages to say that she will enjoy meeting Charles Wilcox but declines to disappoint her aunt by cutting short her visit. He dismisses her interest in the folklore of Howards End.

Helen is less accommodating. She is not willing to let Henry evade responsibility for Leonard's move. When he disparages her ideas about reform and equality, we hear an echo of earlier times when Helen enjoyed being contradicted by the superior arguments of the Wilcoxes. Henry's appeal to immutable laws, which have happily led to progress, are met by Helen's scornful retort that the God of such a universe must have a special concern for the rich. Mr Wilcox believes in a convenient form of Social Darwinism, which allows him to think that only the unfit fail to survive in the battle for life. As the tension and sadness increase, Forster makes first Helen, then Margaret, look out at the sea, which seems to stand for all that has been disagreeable in this episode. Margaret decides to go away with Henry, although she is yielding to his pressure and disappointing her aunt. Does the 'wave of tenderness' for him that comes over her continue the unhappy associations of sea imagery we have noticed?. And can we feel sure that Margaret is right in not being disquieted by the emptiness that seems to lie behind Mr Wilcox's 'black, bright eyes' and 'competent stare'.

CHAPTER 23

Summary
Margaret does not leave Swanage without scolding Helen for disapproving of her engagement. Helen then tells her to go ahead with her marriage. She thinks Margaret is brave to attempt to make a relationship with Henry Wilcox. But she intends to go her own way. She will not compromise with Henry or with Tibby. Only her love for Margaret is unchangeable. Margaret thinks Helen too extreme; her

own way is to seek a balance between the practical and the mystical. She asks Helen to be civil to Henry in company, and returns to London satisfied that their relationship is intact. Next day, she goes to Henry's office. Charles and Henry talk disparagingly about the tenant of Howards End before Margaret and Henry leave to visit it. Margaret dislikes travelling by motor-car; it is impossible to see the countryside, and she thinks the car is dangerous. They lunch with Charles'swife, then go to Howards End. It is locked. As Henry goes for a key, Margaret admires the garden. Sheltering from the rain, she finds the house is open after all. She finds it uncared for, but she has regained a sense of space which London seemed to have deprived her. Hearing a noise in the house, she throws open a door to the stairs. An old woman comes down them, who tells her she resembles Mrs Wilcox.

Commentary
Having avoided an estrangement with Helen, Margaret is thrust into the business and domestic worlds of the Wilcoxes. Forster's description of Mr Wilcox's office emphasises its disorder and lack of human dignity. The 'helping of West Africa', depicted on one map, is matched by another where the coninent looks 'like a whale marked out for blubber'. Henry's brand of imperialism is clearly exploitative. Charles and Henry have no time for the personality of the tenant of Howards End. He is merely a legal category.

Margaret is whisked towards Howards End in a car, a mode of transport she detests. Forster once again uses landscape – and, in particular, rivers – to suggest inwardness and repose. The rivers are portrayed as dishevelled nymphs averting their faces from London which is the source of their distress. He accepts that they cannot be as they were in the time of Michael Drayton (1563–1631) who wrote the poem, *Poly-Olbion*, in celebration of the landscape of Great Britain, but they still represent values which should be preserved. Left on her own at Howards End, Margaret has leisure to look at the trees and hedges and spring flowers. It is so different from the world of London offices that Margaret can almost imagine that there is no connection between them:

> She must have interviewed Charles in another world – where one did have interviews. How Helen would revel in such a notion! Charles dead, all people dead, nothing alive but houses and gardens. The obvious dead, the intangible alive, and – no connexion at all between them! Margaret smiled. Would that her own fancies were as clear cut! Would that she could deal as high-handedly with the world!

Although she attributes the fancy to Helen, it is her own. Although she smiles at the idea that the world can be dealt with so drastically, when she lays her hand on the door, she finds it unocked. It is almost as if her 'fancy' has been a kind of key. She thinks of the house as a place where 'children could play and friends shelter from the rain'. There is no mention of husbands or of 'difficult relationships'. The house itself, which Henry (in Chapter 15) called 'impossibly small', restores her sense of the space that is necessary for civilised living.

Two paired paragraphs present contrasting pictures of her recent experience: Helen's warning that she could lose something if she married Henry seems negated by the possibility of gaining Howards End. But her memory of her mixed ancestry and her connection with English and German expansionism is more elusive. Thoughts of the Wilcoxes and of her father collide in her brain; her combined English and German ancestry has 'warmed her blood, but . . . cooled her brain'. Whatever heredity has made her, the old woman who descends the stairs with an eerie unexpectedness sees her as Ruth Wilcox.

CHAPTER 24

Summary
The old woman is Miss Avery who was a friend of Mrs Wilcox. Henry, hearing what has happened, is protective since he believes Margaret has been frightened. He has shown Margaret round Howards End, explaining how he rescued and improved the property which had been left to Mrs Wilcox and her grandmother. Margaret is specially impressed by the wych-elm which appears to bend over the house like a comrade. It seems to her a symbol of a true relationship. It also has the pigs' teeth which Mrs Wilcox had told her about. When Margaret returns to Wickham Place that night, the memory of Howards End evokes from her a love of England she has never known before.

Commentary
Unlike the Wilcox women, Margaret – so Mr Wilcox believes – suffers from 'nerves': he is accordingly protective. His description of her 'clutching a bunch of weeds' reminds us, surely, of Mrs Wilcox with her wisp of hay, and the link between them is strengthened. Margaret bridles when Henry describes Miss Avery as belonging to the uneducated classes and compares her with Dolly, to Dolly's disadvantage. Henry's interest in places is purely practical: the six Danish tumuli are 'curious mounds' and Howards End is too small to pay. Small-scale farming is 'philanthropic bunkum'. Margaret's contact with the house and garden has been touched with magic.

The house and the wych-elm symbolise 'truer relationships' and 'hope on this side of the grave' – phrases which first occurred to Margaret as she meditated on Mrs Wilcox's death (Chapter 12). The possibilities for human life, which she first sensed then, seem to have found a symbol in the comradely relationship of house and tree.

CHAPTER 25

Summary

Evie Wilcox, upset at first by her father's engagement, has become reconciled to it. Margaret finds she is expected to go to Evie's wedding where she will meet Henry's friends. She travels to Mr Wilcox's country house at Oniton where the wedding is to take place. Margaret leaves London with Evie and six of the guests. At Shrewsbury, they are met by Charles and taken by car to Oniton. As they approach Henry's house, the car, in which Margaret is travelling, hits an animal. The women are hastily moved into the following car, leaving the men to deal with the animal's owner. Margaret insists on going back. In jumping out of Charles's car she hurts her hand. One of the men tells her it was only a cat, whose owner will be compensated. On arrival at Oniton Margaret makes light of the incident. Charles and his father put it down to 'nerves'. Charles distrusts Margaret and suspects her intentions. He is afraid she will make him poor. Margaret has other thoughts: stumbling about in the darkness outside, she calls out how much she loves Shropshire and how she hates London. Hearing her, Charles thinks she means mischief.

Commentary

The chapter begins with Evie's dislike and suspicion of Margaret and ends with a similar account of Charles. Forster makes it clear that Henry does not value friendship as the Schlegels do. Margaret 'never forgot anyone for whom she had once cared; she connected, though the connection might be bitter', and she hopes Henry will do the same. Mr Wilcox values places with as little sentiment as he values people. Oniton now turns out to be the wrong place for him, though Margaret is immediately attracted to its size and remoteness. Despite the fact that the guests are not her sort, Margaret does not find them objectionable. But the events recorded in the chapter remind us of the gulf that lies between men and women in this society. The deference women are paid masks a settled assumption of male superiority. Margaret's leap from the car is as much a rejection of sexual subservience as concern for the injured animal.

It is perhaps significant that the accident occurs just after they have seen Oniton for the first time. Margaret's visit to Oniton is a valuable experience for her, but it is also a false start. It marks a breach between her and the Wilcoxes at the same time as it brings her nearer to the place she has long hoped for. Her challenge to Charles – 'Saxon or Celt?' – is an addition to the list of contraries with which we have become familiar. But the surroundings of Oniton have had nothing to say to Charles Wilcox who remains impenetrably Anglo-Saxon.

CHAPTER 26

Summary
Next morning Margaret is delighted by Oniton and looks forward to living there. She idly watches some of the men who are about to bathe in the river. She is summoned to inspect Evie's wedding dress. Then she invites Henry to talk to her. He has little to talk of except business matters: they go down to look at the wine-cellar, while preparations for the wedding go on in the kitchen. The wedding ceremony takes place, followed by the reception. Margaret thinks such preparations would be too much for her own family; Henry suggests they should be married in a hotel. Three unexpected visitors arrive; they turn out to be Helen and Mr and Mrs Bast. Leonard has lost his job and is destitute. Margaret wishes to protect Mr Wilcox from them. She persuades Helen to take the Basts to a hotel, while she asks Henry if he can find a job for Leonard. He agrees to see Leonard, but, meeting Mrs Bast by chance, is recognised by her as a former lover. Henry is upset and ashamed. He thinks the Basts have been brought to disgrace him and that his engagement to Margaret is at an end. But she decides the matter is not her concern: it had happened during the late Mrs Wilcox's lifetime.

Commentary
This chapter is a test of Margaret's sincerity and integrity. Its focus is on her loving optimism: she is fascinated by Oniton and hopeful about Henry. She has a strong feeling for the house and its setting. Its situation 'thrilled her with poetry' – a word which has not been much used in the novel, but which signifies as positive a value as the word 'joy' which follows it. The 'joy' is caused by a beautiful view–the prospect of hills ('rounded Druids') and rivers which bring with them intimations of Celtic mystery. Margaret hopes Oniton will be a house where she can 'create new sanctities' to replace what she has lost in Wickham Place.

We have, of course, already been warned (in Chapter 25) that 'Oniton was to prove one of her innumerable false starts'. It is not surprising that her mood of optimism should be attenuated by the trivialities which drain Evie's wedding of significance. Forster knits together a succession of unimportant events which, taken together, depress our faith in Margaret's vision: the men fuss and are prudish when they catch sight of her as they prepare to bathe in the river; the wedding is well-managed but meaningless; Henry has nothing to say to her when she expects him to speak personally. She believes her love will help him to become human, but it is all too obvious how little response Henry makes. It is soon clear, indeed, that more will be expected of Margaret. The exaggerated chivalry of men of Henry's type is simply a sign of their sense of superiority. It brings Henry and his butler together when she says something that makes them smile. Instead of claiming equality, she begins to count it a success that she 'has made a special point of kow-towing to the men'. When we read that 'they were breaking camp that night' we sense that Margaret has almost allowed herself to adopt the role of the squaw, whose business it is to see that the men are properly looked after.

Just before Helen and the Basts arrive, Margaret has another glimpse of the landscape which has been the source of her optimism. The 'swirling gold' of the river 'was pouring towards them' but it has to pass 'Charles's bathing shed!' The intrusions of the Wilcoxes into the countryside are matched by the arrival of the Basts who carry with them reminders of the abyss. Margaret's dazzled vision of the golden river gives way to the reality of an angry sister, an out-of-work clerk and his disreputable wife. Margaret manages them with common sense, tact and stubbornly rational argument. She refuses to become emotional or to talk of duty. Her main aim in dealing with the situation is to protect Henry. When Henry appears on the scene, she manages him, too, by using a persuasiveness which is essentially an admission of subservience.

> She was ashamed of her own diplomacy. In dealing with a Wilcox, how tempting it was to lapse from comradeship, and give him the kind of woman he desired.

'Comradeship' is a term that finds the root of love and marriage in the friendship of equals, but the Wilcoxes have no time for such a notion. In persuading Henry to consider giving Leonard a job, Margaret is reduced to using all the arts that women have traditionally used to influence their men. Now she looks at Oniton with different eyes: its ruinous state stands for the compromise that has to be made between ideal and reality. Margaret's initial confidence in the transforming power of her love seems to have dwindled to a willingness to settle for compromise.

The final episode of the chapter tests her forbearance to the limit. His disreputable past melodramatically exposed, Henry projects his guilt feelings on to her: somehow she has used the Basts to expose him. She is protected by her innocence and her steadfastness. When she learns the truth, she persuades herself that it does not concern her, since it took place in the lifetime of Mrs Wilcox. But at this stage of the novel can Margaret so easily dissociate herself from her predecessor?

CHAPTER 27

Summary
After taking the Basts to a local hotel, Helen tries to explain to Leonard the difference between those who believe in the personal life, and accept responsibility for their actions, and those who do not. Leonard hopes that he belongs to the former category. He likes Helen's friendliness and contrasts her with Margaret. He does not want Helen to know the truth about Mr Wilcox and Jacky, who is now upstairs in bed. Helen asks him what kind of woman Jacky is. She learns that Leonard's family is ashamed of her and that she has been unfaithful to him. Leonard declares that he has given up his idealism: all that matters is money. Helen says that the fact of death makes us realise that life demands to be lived by non-material values, if it is to be worth living at all. People like the Wilcoxes whose aim is to extend the empire of the material are defeated by death. Only love can conquer death, as men discover when they acknowledge they are mortal. A maid brings them letters, written to them by Margaret, which are described in the following chapter.

Commentary
The events of the evening are characteristically described as 'a wave of excitement'. The arrival of the trio releases forces which have quite unimagined consequences. Though Foster does not use the word, their arrival at Oniton is a 'collision' whose effects are about to begin. Although one of them will be Helen's pregnancy, the subject matter of this chapter is almost wholly abstract and theoretical. Helen takes the lead in talking about personal responsibility. People – like the Wilcoxes – who reach beyond the personal are soulless and mechanical, summed up essentially in Helen's phrase, 'panic and emptiness'. Opposed to them are those who say 'I'. Perhaps the reader will be reminded at this point of Leonard's stammered, 'I – I' in Chapter 14, when he was described as a man 'looking for a real home'. Now he has abandoned that identity. He is ashamed of his connection with the country and is interested only in money and in settling down. Now Helen introduces her aphorism, 'Death destroys a man; the idea of Death saves him'. Helen's argument is that Death terrifies the materialist – the 'sane, sound Englishmen, building up empi-

res' – since material things perish. The knowledge that men must die ought to divert their energy towards the non-material. Love, the central force of life, will choose its objects more carefully from among those least subject to decay. Helen's 'paradox' is perhaps best read as an answer to the question first raised at Mrs Wilcox's funeral in Chapter 11 and again in the vision of England in Chapter 19: to what end does the individual or the nation sail towards infinity?

However metaphysical, Helen's thesis about how life should be lived is not doctrinal. It is merely 'the vague yet convincing plea that the Invisible lodges against the Visible'. But it is not clear from the narrative comment how far we should follow her. We are told 'her excitement grew as she tried to cut the rope that fastened Leonard to the Earth'. But, 'Woven of bitter experience, it resisted her'.

Forster has often been criticised for the implausibility of the sexual encounter we presume must follow their reading of Margaret's letters. It is the only attempt he makes in this novel to see whether fulfilled heterosexual love could be a type of the love that Helen has recommended. But is it so surprising that Helen and Leonard should feel that love of this kind was their only resource that night? And would that belief not be confirmed by the 'murmurings of the river' to which they were listening? Or is this an episode, like her love-affair with Paul, another of Helen's innumerable false starts?

CHAPTER 28

Summary
Some hours after her encounter with Helen and the Basts, Margaret writes to Henry in forgiveness. But she feels oppressed by what he has done; it is difficult for her to imagine how men could be so tempted. Comradeship seemed impossible; only the most functional sexual relationship seemed to bring men and women together. She still believes in the possibility of love, but not for herself. She tears up her letter to Henry, then writes one to Leonard Bast, telling him that Henry cannot find him a job. She also writes to Helen urging her to abandon the Basts and join her. She meets Henry and tells him she has invited Helen to come to them. They behave as if nothing has happened. Recovering, Margaret reflects that Henry is no worse than she would have expected. She still loves him and believes he can be redeemed by the power of her love.

Commentary
This chapter movingly displays the power and resilience of Margaret's affection, but its initial paragraphs show how close to despair she has come. She is aware of how careful she is to preserve the inferiority Henry expects from her as a woman. Male and female

seem to have nothing in common but an ignoble sexual attraction; yet Margaret still believes that human beings have transformed this necessary biological function into something more admirable and precious. But the events of the evening have made it impossible to have faith in her belief. She is willing to put Leonard off with a polite fib. Her letter to Helen, though practical, is brutal about the Basts. When she talks to Henry she avoids any talk of feeling, and in doing so fails to give him any opportunity to talk about himself. Though she falls asleep, 'tethered by affection, and lulled by the murmurs of the river that descended all the night from Wales', we may wonder whether she has dealt justly with the people involved. She 'felt herself at one with her future home, colouring it and coloured by it', but there is to be no future for her at Oniton. Has her love for Henry re-asserted itself, or is she simply keeping up appearances?

CHAPTER 29

Summary
Next morning Margaret discusses what has happened with Henry. He tries to suggest he is too bad to be her husband, and is rather annoyed by her calmness. He tries to suggest that women like her cannot understand the temptations suffered by men. She tells him it makes no difference. She sees that Henry is still attempting to avoid making contact with her, because he believes that men and women cannot understand one another. It appears that Helen has not come to spend the night in their house, as Margaret had asked her to. Margaret is afraid she will gossip with Mrs Bast. Henry is resigned to things coming out. He tells Margaret how he had met Jacky in Cyprus, while he was on business there. Margaret assures Henry that she has forgiven him. She goes to the hotel where Helen has been staying, only to find that she and the Basts have gone. Henry has recovered himself. He never wants to hear Jacky spoken of again. They leave Oniton. Although Margaret thinks of it with emotion, she is never to see it again.

Commentary
This chapter closely follows the action of the previous one. Margaret makes a renewed effort at honesty in trying to get Henry to face the sexual misdemeanours he is ashamed of. But Henry can only think in stereotypes. Margaret has too many qualities he prefers to think masculine, though he cannot match her clarity of thought. Henry prefers to be thought intolerable rather than to see himself honestly. He has considerable powers of self-dramatisation. He is full of self-pity and refuses to accept responsibility for the hurt he has done to his late wife. Margaret's wish to mention Mrs Wilcox points

forward to the climax of their relationship in Chapter 38. Henry soon regains control. If necessary, he will lie about Jacky to save his public reputation. Margaret is caught up in the machinery of Henry's arrangements; she fears she may also be compelled to lie for him. Henry has regained his self-control; the past has no power to hurt him. Only the last five minutes matter to him. But the grass which trickles through Margaret's fingers sets her apart from him and links her to the first Mrs Wilcox. The practical effect of her love for Henry has been to make her his accomplice. As they leave Oniton, the hill that obscures her view of 'Charles's new springboard' seems to obliterate the fact that Wilcoxes have ever been there.

CHAPTER 30

Summary
Helen arrives at Oxford to tell Tibby that she is going to Germany. She tells him that she has found out something about Mr Wilcox, who has behaved badly and has ruined the lives of others. She does not want to tell Margaret what she knows. Helen believes that Mr Wilcox had ordered Margaret to write telling the Basts to go. Tibby agrees that Mr Wilcox has behaved badly, though he is not inclined to become involved. Helen tells him that she intends to pay the Basts five thousand pounds in compensation for the damage done to Leonard's professional prospects. Next day Tibby sees Margaret and tells her about Helen's visit. He sends a cheque to Leonard which is returned. When Helen asks Tibby to visit the Basts, he finds they have been evicted for not paying the rent.

Commentary
Forster shifts the point of view in this chapter. The central figure is Tibby; for a short space we see the world from his comfortable lodgings. Forster is just to his merits, but he makes it clear that his outlook is limited. He has interests of his own, but they do not extend much beyond himself. He notices that his sister has changed. She has 'a look of appeal, pathetic yet dignified – the look of a sailor who has lost everything at sea'. But Tibby's attention is given to lunch. Many of the details of the scene help to guide the reader's judgement: Tibby's Chinese grammar underlines his remoteness from the everyday world. Oxford, we are told, 'dreamed and rustled outside', as if Tibby's world were turned in on itself, absorbed in its own mysterious movements. In the sunlight 'the little fire was coated with grey', as if, in comparison with the natural world, Tibby's study lacks warmth. Helen's pathetic story is 'odd'. Tibby shows no curiosity about what his sister has to say. He looks at her 'curiously' when she sobs. Helen's tears were 'nearer the things that did concern him, such as

music' but he is only aware that they are 'unusual'. Tibby's detachment is chilling. Helen's commission to decide whether Margaret should be told what she knows about Mr Wilcox is received coldly. Tibby only becomes animated when he hears how much Helen proposes to give Leonard Bast.

At the end of the chapter Tibby is returned to his state of refined inaction. The contemplation of Oxford's architectural beauty is a perpetual refreshment to him, but the narrator suggests it is too perfect to represent the spirit of England. Tibby only finds it possible to deal with Helen by assimilating her to the figure of the Virgin in the University Church. This beautifully composed chapter exactly places the value of human predicaments when looked at from a purely aesthetic point of view. The Basts are reduced to 'a scurf of books and china ornaments', presumably as worthless as the lives they represent. It is an interesting detail that Tibby uses the word 'haycocks' when he means 'muddles' or 'confusions', although by this time the reader has learned to attach a peculiar significance to hay.

CHAPTER 31

Summary

By September, Wickham Place has been abandoned; the furniture is removed to Howards End for storage. Margaret and Henry are married quietly but, though they spend their honeymoon in Germany, Helen fails to meet them. Mr Wilcox is pleased with Margaret, but she is disappointed to learn that Oniton Grange has been let. At Henry's suggestion, they spend the winter in London, meaning to look for a house in the spring. Margaret enjoys looking after Henry, but she goes about less, and becomes more solitary and more reflective. She finds she is now less interested in words than in things.

Commentary

This chapter begins with the Schlegels' departure from Wickham Place: the end of the house and the break-up of the family are a kind of death. Margaret's life is in transition: the life she moves into is fashioned according to Henry's wishes. She is 'lively and intelligent, and yet so submissive'. Her intellectual interests appear to him the agreeable attractions that a man might expect his wife to have. They enhance his sense of importance, and can always be set aside when they are in danger of getting in the way.

Forster organises the chapter so that the debate between the Wilcoxes about where they are to live is framed by two paragraphs of narrative. The first, written from Henry's point of view, describes his feelings for Margaret in proprietorial tones. He values her as a decoration, a recreation. But essentially she is his inferior. It may be amusing to play at fighting with her but she can never win, for whereas men have 'muscles', women have 'nerves'.

What Margaret's 'nerves' amount to is displayed in the scene that follows. She makes light of her deep feelings for Oniton. Henry complains of the damp; its river, which Forster made much of in previous chapters, is to him 'detestable', 'steaming all night like a kettle'. Margaret's unhappiness is expressed in irony or marked by silence. The uncertainty about where they are to live recalls the narrative to the theme of formlessness and disorder, constantly represented in the novel by London. In a future where people have been deprived of roots, only love will bind them together. The tone of the narrative casts doubts on whether such personal attachment will be sufficient.

Margaret ends by accepting Henry's view of things: her submissiveness seems like a defeat, but her withdrawal from former interests is a move in a new direction: for the second time in the novel we are told of her interest in theosophy.

CHAPTER 32

Summary
On a day in the following spring, Charles Wilcox's wife, Dolly, arrives as Margaret is looking at plans of the house Mr Wilcox intends to build in Sussex. She asks about Helen who has been away from England for eight months; she then tells Margaret that Miss Avery has been unpacking cases at Howards End. It appears that relations between the Wilcoxes and Miss Avery have been strained since Evie sent back a wedding present she had thought was too expensive. Margaret decides to go down to Howards End to see for herself.

Commentary
On the face of it, this chapter merely offers a reason for Margaret's visit to Howards End. Forster adds a suggestion that Margaret has taken a further step away from her inclinations by contemplating moving to an obviously rather extravagant house which is to be built for them. Dolly's visit is fuelled by Charles's jealous anger that his father's money is not being spent on his family. Dolly's envy of the new house is obvious: she appears to suspect something is being concealed from her. Forster makes a careful point of mentioning the length of time Helen has been abroad and underlines the hint by linking her departure to the birth of Dolly's latest child. The reference to Miss Avery as a quarrelsome 'farm-woman' is in contrast to her earlier description in Chapter 24 as someone who might have married the late Mrs Wilcox's brother. Margaret is more likely to be

right in seeing her friendship with Mrs Wilcox as the reason for her expensive wedding present to Evie. The snobbish and suspicious reaction of the Wilcoxes to the gift is a good example of their meanness of spirit. It is also clear that Mr Wilcox is quite prepared to use people, even if he has no great opinion of them. Miss Avery is a member of 'the lower classes', and suitable for exploitation.

CHAPTER 33

Summary
Margaret arrives at Hilton, the village in which Howards End is situated. She goes by way of Miss Avery's farm through beautiful countryside. Miss Avery's niece officiously accompanies her to Howards End, where her aunt is waiting. The house appears altered. Miss Avery greets Margaret from inside but does not appear until her niece has gone. When she enters the house, Margaret is astonished to find that it has been furnished with items from Wickham Place. Margaret explains that Mr Wilcox does not intend to live at Howards End, but Miss Avery is not convinced. She wonders if he is afraid of hay fever. Margaret attempts to defend the Wilcoxes from the old lady's implied criticism. Miss Avery says that the late Mrs Wilcox should have married a soldier. Margaret insists that she does not intend to return to Howards End, but she decides to consult Henry before giving orders that the furniture should be put back into store.

Commentary
Margaret's visit to Howards End prepares the way for the culminating events of the novel. Forster treats her walk from the station to the farm in considerable detail. Margaret walks through an avenue of chestnuts which 'must have been planted by the angels', but the church to which it leads does not interest Forster. He is more interested in the 'untouched country' to which it brings Margaret. Forster thinks of it as unpossessed by great landowners or by suburban householders; it is free. The human relationship it suggests is 'comradeship' – a comradeship 'not passionate'. We are to suppose, perhaps, some intimate relationship undisturbed by sex. If Forster is laying a trail for such a relationship, he is not ready to reveal it yet.

Any suggestion of perfect harmony in Margaret's communion with the countryside is eliminated when she meets Miss Avery's niece whose false good manners assert a social equality her obsequiousness denies. The honest farm-house's best parlour has been improved

(Forster means 'spoiled') by decoration in the newest style. But the place suggests stability and rootedness. Implicit in the commentary is the suggestion that human life and the countryside are in a natural relationship. If the farm-house suggests sadness, it is a sadness appropriate to human experience. In these passages, Forster seems to share Wordsworth's belief in the special value of living in the country. There it may be possible to gain a comprehensive understanding of human existence, which may lead to sympathy with others and the development of a sense of brotherhood. Here in the countryside, Margaret feels the strength of the appeal of the sights and sounds of the natural world which are so vividly sensuous as to evoke the presence of a goddess, the Spirit of Spring, as embodied in paint by Botticelli.

After such lyricism, Forster returns to ironic comedy. Miss Avery whom they meet at Howards End is touched with fey astringency. She is a sardonic white witch, a keen-eyed, sharp-witted, fortune-teller. To her niece, is she 'so odd at times'? For the time being she is the appropriate spirit of the place, a temporary guardian preparing for the arrival of the rightful owner. She takes up Margaret's suggestion that a mistake has been made, extending it into the past history of the marriage between the then Miss Howard and Henry Wilcox. Her mention of the hay fever which afflicts the Wilcox men is another reminder of their incompatibility with the values of the countryside. Her placing of Tibby's old crib in the room Helen used when she stayed there may be another of Forster's clues to Helen's present condition, though Margaret takes it as a commment on her own probable childlessness. Miss Avery's words and the atmosphere of the house test Margaret's loyalty to the Wilcoxes. Her affirmation of the rightness of the world, 'so long as men like my husband and his sons govern it', is only faintly echoed by Miss Avery. Henry Wilcox, however suited to Margaret, is not the 'real soldier' whom Ruth Wilcox should have married. Such men, for the purposes of this novel, seem to be buried in the six Danish tumuli that stand on the high road that leads to Hilton station. (It is, of course, a fact that Margaret's father had been a soldier.)

The visit ends with Miss Avery in prophetic mood: 'A better time is coming now, though you've kept me long enough waiting. In a couple of weeks I'll see your lights shining through the hedge of an evening. Have you ordered in coals?' These are the tones and cadences of the poetic spaewife in a play by Yeats or Synge. The smooth metre of the first sentence conveys the assurance of inspired prediction: the luminous vision of houselights through the hedge has all the simplicity of clairvoyance. But when Margaret asks her to hand over the keys of the house, Forster easily returns Miss Avery to the role of the dutiful housekeeper.

CHAPTER 34

Summary

Aunt Juley falls ill. Margaret and Tibby go to see her and send a message to Helen. She recovers, but the puzzle of Helen's absence remains. Margaret wonders if she has been permanently damaged by her encounter with Paul Wilcox. Helen writes to say that she will return to London but may only be contacted through her bank. She will come to Swanage if Aunt Juley is ill enough to need her. When Margaret informs her that Aunt Juley is better, Helen writes to ask where their furniture is, since she wants some books. Margaret tries to force Helen to meet her but without success. She asks Henry's advice, thinking that Helen's behaviour suggests she is mad. He suggests they tell Helen that her books are at Howards End, but that she must collect them herself. Then they can waylay her. Although she dislikes this plan, Margaret writes to Helen naming a day for her visit, suggesting that a charwoman will open the house. Charles, who dislikes the plan for other reasons, warns his father that he may be courting danger.

Commentary

The easy, conversational style of the ending of the previous chapter is maintained at the beginning of this one. As the narrator begins to describe the detail of Margaret and Tibby's visit to Swanage the tone changes: on a day which seems inappropriately perfect and when the approach of the waves to the shore seems self-effacing, Forster begins a meditation on death. There is no heroism or mystery about Aunt Juley's apparently imminent death. She puts in question Helen's paradox about death, since its approach evokes from her no new quality of thought or action: she does not cease to occupy herself with trifles. The contrast between Helen and Margaret is sharply made: Margaret sees 'Death stripped of any false romance; whatever the idea of Death may contain, the process can be trivial and hideous'.

In fact, of course, Aunt Juley does not die. Unfathomable forces of life restore her. Margaret's attention turns to Helen, and this chapter and the seven that follow trace the consequences of her concern. These chapters are dense with incident, some of them surprisingly melodramatic. The incidents themselves have a closer causal link than those that precede them. They do not exemplify the ebb and flow of chance and coincidence. They demonstrate the rapid march of linked events and the explosion which can be produced when two such causal chains collide.

Despite the overt support which the narrative commentary gives to Margaret, the action shows her under pressure to betray her own insights. Margaret's first position is admirable enough. She declines to entice Helen to Swanage, even if in doing so she might be acting for the best. Helen's disappearance has affected Margaret deeply. The breaking of the bond of trust, of affection and open communication, suggests something worse than death: 'Helen had passed into chaos'. It is a state mirrored by London with its 'slowly – flowing slabs of mud', a striking image of the disintegration which threatens human culture. Margaret takes refuge in St. Paul's for a moment, but the perfection of its architecture is only external: inside it is as formless as the London streets, consisting of 'echoes and whispers, inaudible songs, invisible mosaics, wet footmarks crossing and recrossing the floor'.

When Margaret turns to Henry for help he suggests a deception in which personal relations count for nothing. As Forster puts it: '[Henry] was determined to push the matter to a satisfactory conclusion, and Helen faded as he talked. Her fair, flying hair and eager eyes counted for nothing, for she was ill, without rights, and any of her friends might hunt her'. The sentence is a good example of Forster's steely irony. It is offered with a plausibility which the reader might just not notice he is being invited to challenge. The sentence that follows – 'Sick at heart, Margaret joined in the chase' – shows that Margaret has felt correctly about Henry's plan but has mistakenly followed his advice. How far does this throw some retrospective light on the narrator's earlier commendation of Margaret's success – 'so far as success is yet possible' – in 'digesting her own soul'?

CHAPTER 35

Summary
On the day that Helen is to go to Howards End, Margaret and Henry go to Hilton. A message reaches them that Helen is on her way. With many misgivings Margaret goes to the house, having just managed to prevent Henry going on his own. They pick up a doctor on the way. They find Helen in the porch of Howards End. When Margaret sees her, she knows that Helen's trouble is not madness. She unlocks the door of the house and pushes Helen inside.

Commentary
It is worth comparing the events of the day described in this chapter with those of Margaret's previous visit. Forster links that morning and this afternoon – both, so beautiful, and described with a fully-committed lyricism, are 'the scales of a single balance'. But another comparison is laid on the scales: that day she had 'spent with Miss Avery'; now she sets out 'to entrap Helen'. Everything is the same: 'man alone, with his schemes and ailments, was troubling Nature until he saw her through a veil of tears'. Forster's generalisation has a

specific reference: it is Margaret who suffers in this chapter from a dimmed and distorted vision. The balance of the phrases 'spent with' and 'set out to entrap' is part of Forster's irony. Could Margaret apply the word 'entrap' to her conscious intention? Can it be used of her without regret?

In the following paragraph we follow Margaret's thoughts more closely. Her acquiescence in Henry's plan is treated with the same grave irony. Each sentence has to be turned over and looked at twice. Is kindness, however admirable, sufficient to serve as a standard for judging action? Why must Margaret trust him 'absolutely'? Does Henry's wish to act well compel her to approve of what he does? Or does her being married to him do so? 'As soon as he had taken up a business, his obtuseness vanished'. The word 'business' rings hollowly, as does 'profited' in the final sentence of the paragraph: 'He profited by the slightest indications, and the capture of Helen promised to be staged as deftly as the marriage of Evie'. 'Business' and 'profit' are followed by 'capture'. Helen is now simply the object of a manipulative exercise. The word 'staged' with its suggestion of artificiality throws a cold enough light on what Evie's marriage has meant to Mr Wilcox. Helen is now the object – or the 'victim' as she is called in the next paragraph – of Henry's business skill. Margaret's bother about what is happening is expressed in gestures of despair.

The instrumental attitude Henry adopts towards Helen is soon turned on Margaret herself, when Henry almost tricks her into being left behind while he continues to pursue Helen alone. 'Doing things for the best' turns out to be a homely way of saying that the end justifies the means. Margaret discovers that as an absolute value, honesty has priority over kindness by seeing the effects of dishonesty when it is practised against herself. Margaret's feelings of unease are changed to anger when a third person (the doctor) is introduced into the chase. In being described, and labelled, Helen is depersonalised, a case for treatment, rather than a person to be given sympathy and love. Margaret's meditations on the question strike a curiously modern note: if her sister is mad, it may be that madness is a condition ascribed to individuals by society. If that is the case, Margaret's course is clear: 'They would be mad together if the world chose to consider them so'. But it is from the social stigma of being pregnant but unmarried that Margaret has to protect her sister.

CHAPTER 36

Summary

Soon Helen's secret is common knowledge: Henry is horrified. Margaret sends the men away. There is no need for a doctor: what

Helen needs is affection. Henry is persuaded to leave, and Margaret asks Helen to forgive her.

Commentary
Margaret's submission to Henry begins to be replaced by a revival of her sense of loyalty to Helen. Forster indicates this change by suggesting Margaret's initial disorientation. She does not behave rationally at first; she responds to the behaviour of Henry and the other men involved according to instincts deeper than reason. Sentences such as, 'She heard him wonder why she had let Helen in' and 'Presently she heard herself speaking. She, or someone for her, said "Go away"'suggest that Margeret has temporarily lost touch with the social world she has chosen and with her conscious self. Her allegiance is no longer to her husband but to her own sex, and to her sister in particular. As we might expect, Henry is slow to realise what is wrong with Helen; when he does so, he applies to her the double sexual standard men have usually applied to women. As the scene proceeds, Margaret regains her incisiveness: all that matters at present is affection. Helen and Margaret's sisterly love gives each of them a claim on the other which goes beyond prudence or professional advice.

CHAPTER 37

Summary
Inside the house, Helen is surprised to find the furniture unpacked. Margaret apologises for the deception. Helen says she cannot now remain in England; she has an Italian friend who will help her. She asks about the house which seems more alive than it did when the Wilcoxes lived there. Margaret explains about Miss Avery's mistake. There is an awkwardness between them. As Helen prepares to leave, she looks at some of the furniture she remembers from Wickham Place. As they look round, they begin to remember the past. They realise that shared experience still has the power to keep them together. A little boy, sent by Miss Avery, brings them milk. Helen suggests that she and Margaret should spend the night in the house, where she feels at home. Despite some hesitation, Margaret goes to Hilton to ask Henry's permission. She has a premonition of tragedy. She has also begun to think that Miss Avery's prophecy about her return to Howards End may be coming true.

Commentary
That Helen says nothing about what happened outside is a sufficient indication of her displeasure. That she asks whether Aunt Juley has been ill indicates how little trust she can now put in what Margaret

has told her. Margaret loses no time in showing her contrition: she has broken faith with her oldest friend. Helen keeps a level tone, objectively explaining what she intends to do and why she cannot remain in England. When she uses the word 'we', Margaret looks away. Presumably, she thinks Helen is referring to the baby's father. Helen, after all, has herself been guilty of a concealment which may imply a want of trust. In fact she is referring to a new woman friend – a 'crude feminist' – but the only friend she has been able to rely on. When she talks to Margaret 'with measured kindness' – as if she had to be careful of a limited supply – it is clear that she has not yet forgiven her. It is only when her attention is fixed by a book – an object they have shared in the past – that some warmth returns. She is able to say, 'I am still Helen, I hope', and she talks of the house being alive. (Margaret has described it as being 'dead; it is only later in the conversation that she recognises it is she who has been so.)

Helen wants to escape from the inflexible censure then heaped on women who had violated conventional morality, but the furniture of Wickham place holds her. She begins to lose some of her hurt self-control; she looks at the emblems of family affection which are there, and remembers what is not. The warmth becomes stronger: together, they move a chair so that it will have a view of the lawn. As they begin to think of incidents in the past which bring them together, the scene gives way to the comments of the narrator:

> They never could be parted because their love was rooted in common things . . . their salvation was lying around them – the past sanctifying the present; the present, with wild heart-throb, declaring that there would after all be a future, with laughter and the voices of children . . . . They looked into each other's eyes. The inner life had paid.

The authorial guidance here is direct and unmistakable. There is no irony; it is an urgent, moved, record of a significant moment of reconciliation. It is a justification of one of the principal articles of Schlegel faith – namely, that personal relationships have special value. In addition, a mystical belief in the power of the past, hitherto expressed indirectly through references to the traces of history in the landscape or through figures such as Mrs Wilcox or Miss Avery, is given emphatic expression. The final sentence is roundly affirmative.

The dialogue that follows is different in character. The arrival of young Tom with the milk introduces a note of fantasy. Helen's speech becomes playful. We begin to hear of 'the wonderful powers' of Howards End which 'kills what is dreadful and makes what is beautiful live'. The furniture of Wickham Place, transported to the country and touched for the first time by the sun, takes on new life.

4

Forster renders the scene in a prose which has the excitement of
childhood or a touch of the poetry which makes us believe in similar
restorations in Prospero's island. Margaret's caution yields to her
sister's self-confidence. Now Helen can justify herself against the
Wilcoxes:

> my life is great and theirs are little . . . I know of things they
> can't know of, and so do you. We *know* that there's poetry. We
> *know* that there's death. They can only take them on hearsay. We
> know this is our house, because it feels ours.

Now, Helen's 'we' includes Margaret. What she is asserting is the
faith of the Schlegels, the belief that what counts as knowledge is
cultivated feeling which is conscious of itself. This kind of knowledge
is the badge of the owners of Howards End. Perhaps it is also the
answer to the question Forster raised in the final sentence of Chapter
19.

CHAPTER 38

Summary
Margaret goes back to Hilton with a sense of foreboding. Henry
begins to ask questions about Helen which embarrass Margaret by
their crassness. He wants Helen to marry her seducer. Margaret
suggests that the man may be married, but Henry fails to grasp the
allusion to himself. She asks if Helen may stay the night at Howards
End. He repeats his earlier suggestion that she should stay at an
hotel. Margaret begins to believe that Henry thinks Helen is not fit to
stay in the house. He talks of what he owes to his children and to the
memory of his first wife. Margaret cannot refrain any longer from
pointing out that Helen's fault is no different from his own: like him,
she has had a lover. She forces him to recognise the resemblance. He
believes she is trying to blackmail him; he refuses her permission to
sleep at Howards End. She leaves the house.

Commentary
Forster's use of the word 'tragedy' signals a climactic development of
the action, but we are left to attend to the sequence of events and to
interpret them as we can. The unreasonableness of Mr Wilcox's state
of mind is indicated by his attitude to Dolly's baby whom he orders to
be wheeled off the scene. 'It was now the turn of Margaret' suggests
that he is in his most masterful mood. He begins by advocating

honesty, but in practice is mealy-mouthed. He is complacent about himself ('I am a man of the world') and condescending to Margaret ('you are a most exceptional woman'). (To another woman, his tone suggests, he would have been unable to speak at all.) It is her awareness of these nuances that makes Margaret blush. When she looks past him towards 'the Six Hills, covered with spring herbage', she is fixing her eye on a view of the country which perhaps suggests an ideal of heroic manliness Mr Wilcox cannot reach.

Their attitudes to Helen's predicament are so different that the gulf between them cannot be ignored. Henry's use of the word 'seducer' is melodramatic, implying a view of the relationship which is not necessarily true. It is all the more insulting that Henry should believe Helen's friends would want her to marry such a man. As we have noticed before, Margaret's initial weakness is replaced by a steely resilience which is partly moral (she is naturally honest) and partly intellectual (she is a sharply intelligent analyst of moral language). Her first attempt to make Henry aware of the resemblance between Helen's position and his own is a failure. She is even afraid of it as an act of violence. ('Her first blow missed.') Its failure allows her to ask him if Helen may stay the night at Howards End. Once more Forster indicates that her request has a crucial significance. For Henry it is a kind of test ('it was the crisis of his life'); on his answer depends the future of their relationship. Margaret is not anxious to push him too far. His lack of understanding is to some extent a resource to her. If her main aim is to effect Helen's wish to stay the night at Howards End, it does not matter whether or not Henry understands why she has made the request. She listens to his arguments but also looks for some small sign of feeling that may have more weight than reasoned argument.

But Margaret does not have complete control over her own feelings. When Henry suggests that it is more important for her to meet Charles than to stay with Helen, her self-control gives way. When she says 'your message to Charles was unnecessary, and I have no desire to meet him', her anger is barely concealed. Anger is followed by sarcasm when she asks if Helen's presence will depreciate the value of Howards End. Thus they are led to look into the gulf of an overt quarrel. Forster makes Margaret step back once more, but only for a moment. Henry's mention of his late wife is more than she can bear. The comparison between Henry and Helen, which she hinted at before, is now made brutally specific. Her outburst in this chapter should be compared with Helen's in Chapter 22. Margaret now makes exactly the same accusation as Helen made then. She tells him he is 'criminally muddled'; she has spoilt him long enough. As Henry turns away from her, he not only drops her hands, he wipes his own on a handkerchief. She turns again to look at the Six Hills for comfort and support.

CHAPTER 39

Summary
Charles Wilcox meets Tibby Schlegel at Mr Wilcox's London house. Charles is anxious to get rid of Helen, whom he regards as a danger to the Wilcoxes. Tibby is not particularly concerned about Helen, but goaded by Charles about his responsibilities as a brother, he remembers his last meeting with Helen and her concern for Leonard Bast. Charles seizes on the name eagerly. Tibby is ashamed that he has broken his word to Helen and revealed her secret.

Commentary
No indication is give of the timing of this interview. On the evidence of what Mr Wilcox says in Chapter 38 it must take place on the afternoon of Helen's visit to Howards End. It is part of Mr Wilcox's effort to 'save Helen's name'.

Forster has chosen Charles Wilcox and Tibby Schlegel to represent the extremes of the qualities associated with their respective families. Tibby shares his sisters' aesthetic interests but has none of the moral and social interests which seem to them inescapably associated with a love of the beautiful. Charles does not appear to have different interests from his father: he is simply more obviously unpleasant, suspicious and narrow-minded. He share his father's vanity and his wish to appear in a good light. He sees the history of the Schlegels' dealings with his family in conspiratorial terms. It is clear to him they mean to seize Howards End.

Tibby's role in the interview is less heroic. He is no less vain than Charles and believes that he deserves his own good fortune. His essentially selfish and introverted nature makes it difficult for him to withstand the aggressive tactics of Charles Wilcox, who only wants a name for the father of Helen's child. Tibby's lack of interest in people, which leads to his inadvertently mentioning Leonard's name, contributes to the chain of events Forster is chronicling. Charles has a vigorous imagination, but he uses it to serve what he takes to be his own interests. His vision of the truth is darkened by his wish to believe ill of the Schlegels. He is even capable of believing that Tibby has permitted Helen to meet Leonard in his own rooms.

CHAPTER 40

Summary
At Howards End Leonard appears to have been forgotten. The sisters are outside beside the tree. Margaret wants to protect Helen, not to blame her. Helen now knows that it was Margaret's – not Henry's – idea to dismiss the Basts, and she agrees that Margaret was

right to protect Henry. She tells Margaret indirectly how her pity for Leonard led her to make love with him at Oniton. Leonard was not to blame. Helen believes that she has now reached stability, and that she understands Margaret's feeling for Henry. Margaret does not reveal her recent quarrel with him; she suggests that only Mrs Wilcox understands and that 'she knows everything'. Helen asks Margaret if she will go with her to Germany, but Margaret does not answer directly. The peacefulness of the evening seems to preclude the making of plans. They fall asleep in Howards End. To Margaret, it seems a strange result of Helen's association with Leonard Bast.

Commentary
The chapter begins and ends with a reference to Leonard, but he plays no part in it. The first paragraph of the chapter throws out a hint that he still has some part to play in the narrative, but for the present he is merely something to be explained away. Leonard, we are told, has not been a person for Helen, but a cause. Her feeling for him, like her feeling for Paul Wilcox, has been superficial, even if its consequences have been more serious. Helen's affection for Leonard has been protective – she had looked into his eyes and found that Henry Wilcox had ruined him morally as well as financially. Her love for him had been born of pity.

The chapter has two functions: it effects a reconciliation between Helen and Margaret; it also suggests a surprising role for the late Mrs Wilcox. It is written from Margaret's point of view. She is the recipient of Helen's confession that she had 'isolated' Henry Wilcox as the sole cause of Leonard's misfortune. In using the word 'isolate', Helen tacitly acknowledges that she has made a mistake. She has failed to 'connect': she had judged Henry narrowly and harshly. That Helen is now willing to see the situation in a different light – and to 'understand' Margaret's feeling for Henry – is ironically contrasted with her ignorance of the breach of understanding that has just taken place between Margaret and Henry. But Helen's 'understanding' does prepare the reader for the final stage of the novel in which some kind of reconciliation between Margaret, Helen and Henry takes place.

That, however, is a matter for later chapters. The principal concern of the present chapter is the establishment of Howards End as the place which might 'relieve life's daily grey, and . . . show that it is grey' (Chapter 16). In the third paragraph Forster introduces a reference to the beauty of the spring evening which is to become the dominant note of the whole chapter. Now, time is reduced to a series of moments, which are attached to the past and hallowed by the house and the wych-elm of which so much has been made during the course of the novel. It is in this context that Margaret recalls Mrs Wilcox. She says to Helen:

I feel that you and I and Henry are only fragments of that woman's mind. She knows everything. She is everything. She is the house, and the tree that leans over it . . . I cannot believe that knowledge such as hers will perish with knowledge such as mine. She knew about realities. She knew when people were in love, though she was not in the room. I don't doubt that she knew when Henry deceived her.

The extraordinary powers attributed to Mrs Wilcox were established early in the novel. In Chapter 3 we are told of her:

She seemed to belong not to the young people and their motor, but to the house, and to the tree that overshadowed it. One knew that she worshipped the past, and that the instinctive wisdom the past can alone bestow had descended upon her – that wisdom to which we give the clumsy name of aristocracy. High-born she might not be. But assuredly she cared about her ancestors, and let them help her.

In the latter passage the 'instinctive wisdom' is spoken of as an inherited tradition. Manners and habits of attention, sensititivity based on feeling, have given Mrs Wilcox insight which surpasses anything which learning and intellectually assimilated culture can bestow. But now – after her death – Forster has endowed her with more powerful, if more mysterious, qualities. It is as if, somewhere in the margin of the novel, she is the patient observer by whose agency all its antinomies are reconciled. Her influence after death has, of course, been part of the action of the novel. Her last wish of bequeathing her house to Margaret has been frustrated, but through Miss Avery her memory has been kept alive. Through Miss Avery once more, the identification of Margaret and Mrs Wilcox has been established. Indeed, immediately after the first of the passages quoted above, Miss Avery in passing calls out to Margaret, 'Good night, Mrs Wilcox'.

But even as she takes Mrs Wilcox's place (beside the house, underneath the tree with its ancient and magical pigs' teeth) Margaret marks the difference between herself and her predecessor. The first Mrs Wilcox has become something like the *genius loci* – the presiding deity and guardian of Howards End – a spirit such as was supposed to guard groves and sacred places in ancient times. Margaret may have come to recognise the power and value of such places, but she cannot yet have that sense of deep-rooted attachment to a place which has been the source of Mrs Wilcox's strength and insight.

She and Helen, however, can benefit from the spiritual refreshment which can come from a complete abandonment of concern for anything but the moment as it passes. Forster draws on imagery which he has already established to suggest the special value of this succession of moments. We remember Margaret's sense of pleasure in Oniton with its castle mound and river. Now the river has been transformed into the flow of time itself:

> The present flowed by them like a stream. The tree rustled. It had made music before they were born, and would continue after their deaths, but its song was of the moment. The tree rustled again. Their senses were sharpened, and they seemed to apprehend life. Life passed. The tree rustled again.

This 'peace of the present, which passes understanding' is to be distinguished from that time in which past, present and future are related as cause to effect, or as intention to outcome. It is a time in which human action has been suspended in favour of a passionate apprehension of the natural world and a passionless sense of unity with a loved companion. In this 'moment out of time', to use a phrase of T. S. Eliot's, Margaret and Helen, the house and the tree, are absorbed into an intense state of unity which offers, perhaps, 'hope on this side of the grave'.

CHAPTER 41

Summary
Leonard Bast has been filled with remorse for his sexual episode with Helen. He does not realise how he has been idealised and how little he really means to her. After her departure he has found himself in serious financial difficulties. He has taken to sponging on his relatives. But he remains clear-headed about what has happened, and is still fond of Jacky. He had seen Margaret by chance in St. Paul's Cathedral (presumably on the occasion recorded in Chapter 34) and had formed a wish to tell her his story and ask her advice. He discovers that Margaret has married Mr Wilcox and tries to see her in London. He is told she is at Howards End. After a restless night, he decides to take the train to Hilton. When he reaches Howards End, Charles Wilcox (whom Leonard has not met) has already arrived. Hearing Leonard's name, Charles seizes him and beats him with a sword which belonged to the late Mr Schlegel. Books fall on Leonard, and he dies.

Commentary
Much of this chapter consists of a summary of Leonard's life since his arrival with Helen and his wife at Oniton. But the recital of events is subordinated to a more striking rhetorical design which converts the psychological agonies of remorse into the literal killing of Leonard by

Charles Wilcox. Forster begins the series of metaphors simply enough by capitalising the word 'remorse', converting it into an allegorical figure, who inflicts punishment on those who have sinned. Forster vividly conveys Leonard's sense of depression and self-blame which affect him as if they were 'brown rain' or 'a burden' or 'little' irons' or 'a sword'. (It is interesting to note that, on Leonard's first appearance in Chapter 6, we are told that 'a sharp pain darted through his head!') At the same time it is suggested that there is something wilful and unhealthy about this inner psychic process which attempts to heal by cutting away parts that offend.

In his present state Leonard is a victim of his own self-absorption. He fails to 'see things steadily and see them whole'; he does not connect; he does not understand himself as part of a larger process. He mistakenly believes he alone is to blame for what has happened. He sees himself as if an outcast from society, as no better than Jacky. These excessive feelings of guilt may be thought to be the antithesis of Henry's inability to feel shame at his own behaviour. External and internal events have reduced Leonard to a shadow of himself. He has lost the spirit which once had prompted him to walk into the countryside at night. Moved by a kind of religious masochism, he hopes to find relief by confessing his sins to Margaret.

But Leonard has not completely succumbed to his mania. As he tosses on his bed, the sight of a patch of moonlight splits off the robustly sceptical common sense, which is a part of him, from his wretchedly tortured self. He looks out of his window and sees the moon, not as a symbol of his guilt, but as part of a tranquil and beautiful world. His journey to Howards End brings him closer to that natural world where the self-inflicted punishments of a diseased self-consciousness have no power. As he moves on, taken out of himself by the beauty of the sun and the flowers and the song of birds, he regains something of the unselfconscious health which his country ancestors had enjoyed. His preoccupation with sin brings him an awareness of goodness and a glimpse of the possibility of joy. Forster leaves Leonard on the threshold of discovering quite different reasons for living than those of reward and punishment. The sword of guilt with which he has punished himself is replaced by the real sword which Charles Wilcox, sure of his right to judge, brings down on Leonard's shoulders.

CHAPTER 42

Summary
After Margaret returns to Howards End on the night before Leonard is killed, Charles Wilcox arrives home from London. His father is concerned at Margaret's absence, and displeased by her disobe-

dience. Charles suggests he will go to Howards End early next morning. He does so, returning to Hilton after Leonard's death, which he believes has been caused by a heart attack. He explains that Margaret had told him she intended to go to Germany with Helen. Then Leonard made his appearance. Charles seems to think he had been hiding in the house with the knowledge of Margaret and her sister. He believes he was justified in tackling Leonard – Mr Schlegel's sword was the nearest thing he could hit him with. Charles fears a scandal, but is happy to think that his father will be free of entanglement with the Schlegels. Mr Wilcox finds out that there is to be an inquest on Leonard which Charles is required to attend.

Commentary

This chapter goes back in time to explain how Charles came to be in Howards End when Leonard arrived there. The centre of interest is Charles: the chapter is suffused with his narrow-minded scorn and his suspicion of the Schlegels. Mr Wilcox displays some of these feelings also. He is strong on property rights; he looks 'angrily at the moon'. When Charles returns with many good reasons for striking Leonard – whose death has been the regrettable consequence of a justifiable thrashing – Mr Wilcox is 'shading his eyes from the sun'. It is as if he is deliberately cutting himself off from the beneficent powers of Nature.

But Charles's story does not quite satisfy his father, who is made anxious by some of its details, particularly by his use of the sword. Charles is afraid of scandal, but he has no fear of his own position. Mr Wilcox's rejection of Charles's offer of a car to take him to the police station may be an indication of a small breach between father and son. Perhaps it is the first sign of a change in his attitude. To Charles, his father's petulance seems 'more like a woman' – as if Charles himself has noticed the change. Charles feels his father may need some replacement for Margaret, but he is unable to express the feeling of affection he has for him. His father returns from the police station 'looking very tired'. Perhaps we are to infer that Charles's display of the Wilcox spirit has made a difference to his father's perception of things.

CHAPTER 43

Summary

At Howards End Margaret despairs of any good emerging from the apparently senseless chain of events that has led to Leonard's death, but she cannot believe that life has nothing more to offer than turmoil and disorder. For one thing, there is Helen's child to look forward to. She answers questions about the circumstances of Leonard's death;

she arranges for Helen to stay at the farmhouse. She does not regret her breach with Henry: it represented a protest against the insensitive blindness of many men. She does not believe she will share Henry's future, but her love for him has not altered. When he sends for her, she reminds him that she intends to go to Germany with Helen, that she cannot forgive him, and intends to leave him. He tells her that Charles is likely to be found guilty of manslaughter. In fact, Charles is sentenced to three years' imprisonment. His defences down at last, Mr Wilcox is a broken man. Margaret takes him to Howards End to recover.

Commentary
In this chapter Forster returns to look at events from Margaret's point of view. The first three paragraphs are written in the style of generalised meditative brooding which is common to Margaret and to the narrative commentary. There is no immediate indication of time and place. Except for 'Here Leonard lay dead in the garden', we are not told that Margaret's thinking is taking place on the morning of Leonard's death and that she is still at Howards End. Margaret's thoughts are focused on 'the unseen': she believes there must be something more than the 'ordered insanity' of the chain of events which has led to Leonard's death and which has been as ordered, but as senseless, as a game of cards.

   In a change of tone, the three following paragraphs sketch a generalised picture of the external events which take place as the doctor and 'officials' investigate the killing. But Margaret's thoughts about the meaning of life and death and about the apparent end of her relationship with Henry continue to occupy the foreground of the chapter. She is satisfied that she was right to confront him with his shortcomings. Her hope, long ago expressed, that 'she might yet be able to help him in the building of the rainbow bridge that should connect the prose in us with the passion' (Chapter 22) seems to have been mistaken. Accepting the breach between them, Margaret withdraws from the current of living. Forster says:

> At such moments the soul retires within, to float upon the bosom of a deeper stream, and has communion with the dead, and sees the world's glory not diminished, but different in kind to what she has supposed. She alters her focus until trivial things are blurred. Margaret had been tending this way all the winter. Leonard's death brought her to the goal. Alas! that Henry should fade away as reality emerged, and only her love for him should remain clear, stamped with his image like the cameos we rescue out of dreams.

Whatever this passage means, Forster is using language rich with religious overtones to suggest a private domain of spiritual values. The altered focus of Margaret's soul links her more firmly to the first Mrs Wilcox, who in Chapter 9 was described as out of focus with daily life: 'one or the other must show blurred'. The world of time, place and causality has been forsaken for a different setting where what is valuable is the form of love itself, whether or not it can be offered to an actual individual. In her mind's eye Margaret follows Henry through his restless and trivial future to his death. They might both live eternally in some future life, but their adherence in this life to quite different values would separate them for ever after death.

When Margaret meets Henry before the chapter ends, things are not as she imagined. Henry cannot understand her dispassionate statement of her plan to leave him. As they sit together on the grass, she learns about Charles's fate, and understands that Henry's defences against feeling are down for ever. As she feels the hill moving beneath her ('as if it was alive'), we understand that a new life has begun for her, just as it had begun for Helen when her baby was conceived. Nothing that follows suggests that Margaret has emerged from the inner spiritual retreat we have been told of earlier, but caring for Mr Wilcox will be one of her future duties. It will be the form her love for him will take.

CHAPTER 44

Summary
More than a year later, Margaret remains at Howards End. Helen is there with her baby and Tom, Miss Avery's grand-nephew, is trying to play with him. Inside the house, the Wilcox family are holding a meeting. Helen and Henry have become friends now, but Helen believes that, in comparison with Margaret, she is unable to love people. Margaret tells her not to worry; people are different and should accept their differences. Helen is grateful to Margaret for salvaging the lives of the people she has cared for. Margaret says she has simply done what has been necessary. When the family meeting breaks up, it appears that Mr Wilcox has decided to leave Howards End to Margaret, who in turn will leave it to Helen's son. As the rest of the family leave, Dolly reveals how the house had once been left to Margaret by Ruth Wilcox. Mr Wilcox explains: the past is forgotten; there are signs that the future will be happy.

Commentary
In the final chapter of the novel, oppositions are resolved by a recognition of the diversity of individual differences and a plea for tolerance. The Wilcoxes – apart from Henry – decide that Howards

End is not a suitable place for them. Even Henry still finds that his hay fever makes it less than comfortable. But it is in the bunch of cut grass that Helen finds an image of the human diversity which Margaret has advised her to rejoice in.

In one way, the ending of the novel is apt and satisfying: Margaret's love for Henry and Helen and Howards End has brought about a reconciliation. The final chapter is tranquil and quietly optimistic. The question of the rivalry of Schlegels and Wilcoxes has been set aside in favour of an acceptance of variety. But in another way, the ending is less satisfactory: the acceptance of diversity scarcely stretches to Evie and Dolly and Paul. Mr Wilcox is now a stricken man whom Margaret has pledged herself to love. When Helen confesses that she no longer believes in the value of 'a woman's love for a man', Margaret disagrees with unusual emphasis, but it is difficult to see that his affirmation carries any sexual connotation. If Margaret has finally found the love which (in Chapter 20) is described as 'a jewel', it is a love which is essentially maternal and protective.

The main benefactors of these events are Tom and baby for whom is predicted a future of friendship. But 'all the same, London's creeping'. Howards End has been established as a supreme value, but will it withstand the encroachment of all that London represents by way of deteriorating standards? Margaret is optimistic that 'this craze for motion' will be followed by a civilisation which will 'rest on the earth'. Seventy years after the first publication of this novel, ecologists and 'friends of the earth', with much greater reason to fear that 'life's going to be melted down, all over the world', may wish to continue to share her faith.

4 THEMES

INTRODUCTION

Howards End is a novel which appears to adhere to the tradition of realism which was the central convention of the nineteenth-century novel, but an interpretation of it which remains at this level is not likely to be convincing. At one level, it is about the interaction of a selected group of people at a given time in given situations, but the selection has been carefully designed to allow the author to explore themes embodied by his characters or brought into focus by their interaction. The novel is set principally in London, but significant scenes take place in the countryside to the north of London at Hilton, the village where Howards End is situated, on the south coast of England at Aunt Juley's home in Swanage, and on the borders to the north-west between England and Wales (Oniton). Each of these places has its own significance: the pattern of contrasts between the characters is repeated in contrasts between places.

The people whose actions are described in the novel comprise three main groups – the Schlegels, the Wilcoxes and the Basts. The two principal characters are Margaret and Helen Schlegel, who form relationships with members of the other groups and with one another. They also interact in a significant way with the places where they live. The novel is about the history of these relationships and about their evolution through time, but at every stage the action of the story implicitly outlines an argument, a critical consideration of the questions raised by the story itself. The novel is mainly seen through Margaret Schlegel's eyes, and, though she is not consciously aware of events in this way, they are most simply described as a quest, a search for what will give her life meaning. She achieves what she is looking for after many false starts. But just what it is she finds is a question which must occupy the attention of everyone who tries to say 'what this work is about'. No explicit account is given by the author of the questions which the novel raises: what they are is open to interpretation. And the same applies to the answers that may be given to them.

4.1 SETTING

Historical time

One consideration which helps to make clear the terms in which the novel may be understood is its historical setting. *Howards End* is set in the early years of the twentieth century. Its historical perspective derives from references made to events and opinions which are supposed to be current at the time the events of the novel are taking place and, more particularly, from references which are made to the personal history of the father of the Schlegel sisters, who had emigrated to England as a result of his dismay at the expansion of his native Prussia and the smaller German states into imperial Germany. This process began with the war Prussia and Austria waged with Denmark in 1864 to remove the Duchies of Schleswig-Holstein from the Kingdom of Denmark. The success of this manoeuvre led two years later to war between Prussia and Austria in which Austria was surprisingly beaten by the Prussian army. Prussia had, at the same time, extended its control over the smaller German states. In 1870, the last stage of this expansion of Prussia into a greater Germany took place when, under Bismarck, German armies were mobilised to fight France. The unification of Germany was achieved in the partiotic heat of war. France was disastrously defeated at the Battle of Sedan on 1 September 1870; the French Emperor was taken prisoner, and the German Empire was proclaimed in Versailles in January 1871. Twenty years later, the Pan-German League aimed at uniting Germans throughout the world into a great German state with an enlarged Germany at its head.

In the fourth chapter of *Howards End* very brief allusions to these events provide the reason for Ernst Schlegel's decision to leave Germany. The only empire of which he wanted to be a citizen was one of intellect and imagination; he had preferred the small German states, such as Weimar, which had nurtured the poet Goethe (1749–1832) or the estates of the semi-autonomous landowners, such as Esterháza, where the composer Haydn (1732–1809) had been employed. But he did not find Britain free from national self-0ggrandisement. As he says to his Prussian nephew, 'Your Pan-Germanism is no more imaginative than our Imperialism here'. From 1870 to 1914 Britain, with its tradition of colonialism, extended its Empire especially in Africa. It had become a dominant commercial and financial power; its adherence to money and material values was a common target for the criticism of novelists such as Dickens, Trollope, Henry James and John Galsworthy. It is perfectly appropriate that Paul Wilcox should take up employment in Nigeria (the Royal Niger Company had been set up in 1896), and that Mr Wilcox's company should be the Imperial and West Africa Company).

It was scarcely to be expected that territorial expansion of this kind could be accomplished without conflict. Germany and Britain had clashed indirectly in South Africa where Germany supported the Dutch-descended farming states against Britain during the Boer War (1899–1902), from which Charles Wilcox had brought back a Dutch bible (Chapter 18). During the early years of the twentieth century Germany had embarked upon becoming 'a commercial Power, . . . a naval Power, . . . with colonies here and a forward policy there, and legitimate aspirations in the other place' (Chapter 4). British politicians had responded by trying to unite the dispersed colonies of the Empire by a system of preferential treatment for goods produced within it. In 1903, Joseph Chamberlain, the principal proponent of these ideas, founded the Tariff Reform League. Margaret Schlegel, a Liberal, who still believes in Free Trade, alludes to these questions in Chapter 25. One of the implicit assumptions of the novel is that Britain and Germany are on course for a collision. As an anonymous clergyman dining in Simpson's says in Chapter 17, 'Their Emperor wants war; well, let him have it'. Although these historical allusions are unobtrusively woven into the fabric of the novel, they do affect its meaning. There is a general aversion to the exercise of power and to aggressive nationalistic expansion. A premonition of destructive conflict in Europe may account for much of the sombreness in *Howards End* and for the earnestness with which the search for saner values is pursued.

4.2 ACTION

No direct connection is made by the novelist between the events of history, sketched out above, and the action of his novel. But it seems reasonable to believe that the careful working out of the fictional events provides a commentary on the historical circumstances in which they are placed. *Howards End* is about a search for values, but it is less clear-cut than the word 'search' suggests. Recent criticism has suggested that it would be wrong to see the novel as the expression of a simple belief in the value of connecting apparently opposing principles and attitudes. A careful scrutiny of the action, and of the attitude of the narrator to it, suggests that the novel means more than the desirability of finding a mean between two extreme positions. The novel's famous epigraph, 'Only connect', should not be taken simply at face-value. It may well be that the point of the novel lies in challenging the reader to decide what it is proper and profitable to attempt to join together. To be more specific, although the novel is very largely written from Margaret Schlegel's point of view, it is not a simple expression of that point of view, but rather a critique of the search for truer values which she engages in.

What Margaret Schlegel thinks she is doing – namely falling in love with, and marrying, Henry Wilcox in order to rescue him from the deficiencies of his type and rehabilitate him as a human being – is rather different from what the novel, taken as a whole, appears to suggest. Margaret believes she is refuting a judgement made by her sister, Helen, in the first chapter of the novel – that the Wilcoxes and the Schlegels are incompatible. The Schlegels represent a social group which can be traced back to the courtiers, advisers and clerks of the Middle Ages: they are intelligent, educated, socially responsible, interested in music, art and the culture of that socially dominant group. The Wilcoxes represent business enterprise, acquisitiveness, and a concern for trade and money-making: they are particularly associated with British Imperialism. In the early chapters of the novel, Margaret accepts that people of her sort are dependent on the commercial skills of people like the Wilcoxes. She therefore believes that some connection can be made between these groups and that her marriage with Henry Wilcox would be an emblem of it. In fact, this connection can hardly be said to take place, certainly not in the strong and optimistic form that Margaret hopes for in Chapter 22. Nothing in *Howards End* persuades the reader to believe that the Wilcoxes as a whole have much to be said for them. The younger men are insensitive and aggressive, overbearing to servants and to women. Indeed, one strongly emphasised theme of the novel is Margaret's resistance to the patronising attitude adopted towards her by the Wilcox men. As the object of her love, Henry Wilcox is temporarily excluded from the harshest judgement, but even Margaret eventually dissociates herself from the partiality and narrowness of his morality, and from his failure of sympathy. She begins to see how far her prejudice in favour of money, which springs from a clear-headed grasp of the essential part it plays in maintaining her own way of life, has led her away from the humane values which her family have traditionally upheld. Her marriage to Henry leads to a partial estrangement from her sister, to which Helen's concealed pregnancy contributes. When Helen's true situation is revealed, Margaret realises that her behaviour towards Helen has been dishonest and disloyal, and that she now wishes to protect her as a woman and as a friend. The night she spends with Helen at Howards End is a recognition of the significance of the values of personal relations and of 'the inner life' which have been a central part of her family tradition.

That night, however, is also the climax of a second line of development in the argument of the novel. From an early point in the novel it has been apparent that London, which is the focus of the intellectual and cultural life which the Schlegels love, is a threat to the kingdom as a whole. In addition to the worlds of liberal culture and of business, there is a third realm – the unspoiled agricultural country-side of England – represented in the novel by Mrs Wilcox and, less fully, by Leonard Bast. Mrs Wilcox, whom Margaret befriends, does not fit into the leisured 'intellectual' world of the Schlegels, and, indeed, causes Margaret to revise her opinion of its value. Leonard Bast, who aspires to share the Schlegels' culture, is in fact a displaced countryman whose instinct to return to it is praised by Helen and Margaret as a move towards reality and truth, although Leonard himself thinks of it as a romantic adventure, unconnected with the everyday world of work. Margaret, having failed initially to join Mrs Wilcox in a visit to her home in the country, Howards End, finds that she has embarked on a search for a new home, which has been stimulated partly by the power she finds in Mrs Wilcox and partly by the expiry of the lease of her London flat. Although Margaret's visits to the countryside begin by chance they develop a pattern which adds new meaning to the novel. She begins to see the beauty of the countryside, not in aesthetic but in moral and spiritual terms. She begins to understand the values represented by Mrs Wilcox, by the superstitions of the countryside, by the memorials of the past, by Howards End itself. Her first unachieved visit to Howards End introduces these themes into the novel; they are continued, and expanded by Leonard Bast's 'adventure', by Margaret's first visit to Howards End, and by her subsequent visit to Oniton. The climax of the series of episodes is reached when she spends the night with Helen at Howards End, where she finds 'the very dear place' and 'they very dear person' which will relieve 'life's daily grey.'

One consequence of Margaret's discovery of the values of the countryside is her gradual identification with the first Mrs Wilcox. Although she at first resists this re-creation of her self, by the end of the novel she has accepted it. Her development does not end with her discovery of 'the very dear place' where she can take root. By the end of the novel everyday life has become as 'blurred' for Margaret as it had been for Ruth Wilcox. She has passed beyond the need for human relationships; if she still believes in love, it does not seem a love which is primarily directed towards other human beings, al-though her protective love for Henry remains. In the last chapter of the novel she seems to have attained a relationship with 'the unseen', which is directly spiritual. Forster almost uses the language of Eastern mysticism to suggest Margaret's escape from the mechanical routine of existence 'to float upon some deeper stream'. In such a state, Forster tells us, 'trivial things are blurred'. Such a phrase was used of the first Mrs Wilcox in Chapter 9, where it was said of her, 'Yet she and daily life were out of focus: one or the other must show blurred'. Whatever this state of mind may be, Forster appears to regard it as valuable and worth attaining. It seems related to the doctrines of Theosophy, which is explicitly referred to three times in the novel as a subject Margaret has studied with interest. Its doctrines of reincarnation may have some relevance to the re-formation of Margaret's spirit according to the pattern of Mrs Wilcox. More pertinently, its doctrines of hierarchically ordered stages of enlightenment, which are explicitly applied by Margaret to Mrs Wilcox and herself in Chapter 40 and to Henry and herself in Chapter 44, suggest perhaps another way of 'connecting'. If Margaret's practical attempt to connect Schlegels and Wilcoxes has failed, it may be that they can be connected at a higher level as part of a pattern of difference of type and individual in which all apparent disparities are reconciled. But such meanings – if indeed they are hinted at in the novel – are only fleetingly implied, though the distancing of Margaret from the human world is clearly indicated.

If the novel ends in optimism about the world 'this side of the grave', that optimism is expressed by Helen and relates to her son and the possibilities of his life. He is the child of Helen Schlegel and Leonard Bast; he has been returned to the countryside from which his father was displaced; and there appears to be for him a possibility of comradeship in the person of Tom, Miss Avery's grand-nephew. By the end of the novel, the Wilcoxes have been eliminated from the scene, except for Henry who is a broken man, dependent on Margaret for love and understanding. For the moment, at least, the feminine principle has triumphed.

Readers must judge for themselves the quality of the optimism of the novel's ending, taking account of the partial withdrawal of Margaret from the scene. More interesting, perhaps, is Forster's general treatment of Helen and the meanings she contributes to the novel. On several occasions it is suggested that we should mistrust her impetuosity and her intransigent belief in absolute values. Yet it is not possible to dismiss Helen as simply hysterical and impractical. Her judgement of the Wilcoxes taken as a whole is not seriously challenged by the events of the novel. Her response to Beethoven's Fifth Symphony in Chapter 5 is given detailed and sympathetic treatment by Forster. Helen sees:

> Gusts of splendour, gods and demi-gods contending with vast swords, colour and fragrance broadcast on the field of battle, magnificent victory, magnificent death! Oh, it all burst before the girl, and she even stretched out her gloved hands as if it was tangible. Any fate was titanic; any contest desirable; conqueror and conquered would alike by applauded by the angels of the utmost stars.
>
> And the goblins – they had not really been there at all? They were only the phantoms of cowardice and unbelief? One healthy human impulse would dispel them? Men like the Wilcoxes, or President Roosevelt, would say yes. Beethoven knew better. The

goblins really had been there. They might return – and they did. It
was as if the splendour of life might boil over and waste to steam
and froth. In its dissolution one heard the terrible, ominous note,
and a goblin, with increased malignity, walked quietly over the
universe from end to end. Panic and emptiness! Panic and
empiness! Even the flaming ramparts of the world might fall.

Here, as in her talk with Leonard in Chapter 27, where she considers
the value of the concept of Death, Helen is taken seriously by her
creator. In both scenes she is called – surely, affectionately – 'the
girl'. However much her impetuosity and intransigence may be
criticised, she has impressive moments of insight which are not
challenged in the novel. She is aware of the existence of Good and
Evil and that Evil is a feature of existence which liberal optimism
cannot eliminate. Equally strongly, she sees the dependence of
positive value on the knowledge that men and women have of the
death of everything they love. In her own way, and at a deeper, if
more abstract, level, she 'connects' – sees the interdependence of the
positive and negative poles of existence. Forster uses Helen to
suggest the content of the speculative and philosophical aspects of his
novel, perhaps because he does not wish to appear to preach. He has
encouraged the reader to discount Helen; he gives her opinions which
are strong enough to make their own point, and yet remain decently
muted in the mind or mouth of a secondary character. Meanwhile,
Margaret, quieter, more pragmatic, carries the main burden of the
action to a conclusion, which is not at variance with her sister's
insights, even if it is less explicit.

The story of Leonard Bast describes a parallel search for true
values which leads him away, on the one hand, from the insubstantial
culture of literature and art to the 'real' culture of country life. As he
moves towards his death, Leonard repudiates the attachment to
materialism which, in despair at Oniton, he had wrongly believed to
be the only worthwhile value for a working man. In doing so, he
brings into question Margaret's theory that, given an adequate
financial base, any kind of life which satisfied individual taste may be
justified. Leonard follows Helen in coming to believe that the fact of
death forces men and women to scrutinise the aims they pursue more
critically: such values must be soundly based and enduring. Honesty,
self-knowledge, love and understanding of others, loyalty, and a
humble awareness of human dependence upon the limited resources
of the Earth are commended; purely aesthetic interests are not
encouraged; aggressive acquisitiveness is deplored. But behind these
fairly simple recommendations, implied by the novel, lie two more
complex, less easily definable, positions: the first is Forster's belief in
the values of the countryside and rural ways of life – a belief which
links him to the nature-worship of Wordsworthian romanticism; the

second, obliquely but persistently alluded to, is a religious mysticism which appears to see life as a journey towards a state of spiritual perfection, where the discordant oppositions of human experience appear as a variegated, but unified, whole.

5 TECHNICAL FEATURES

5.1 THE NARRATIVE STRUCTURE: A GENERAL SUMMARY

The meanings which were discussed in the last section are carried by many features of the structure of the novel. One of these is the arrangement of the events of the novel. Like many novels and short stories, *Howards End* begins with a little episode that establishes in a very simple way some of the major themes of the novel. Thus, Helen discovers her incompatibility with Paul Wilcox and concludes that people like the Wilcoxes cannot connect with people like the Schlegels. Mrs Wilcox is carefully differentiated from the rest of her family by a specific verbal device (her 'wisps of hay' and the hay fever that does not affect her); we conclude that she is to be treated as a separate case. Immediately after this episode, Forster describes the Schlegel sisters in a way which differentiates them from one another and suggests they offer contrasting ways of looking at the world. He then introduces Leonard Bast, the partly-educated devotee of 'culture', who is both part of the Schlegel sisters' story and separate from it, making a distinctive contribution to the meaning of the novel as a whole. Margaret then begins to make friends with Mrs Wilcox. She fails, and Mrs Wilcox dies, but before her death, we are given a first strong indication of the significance her house, Howards End, has for her. It is also clear that she has seen in Margaret, rather than in any member of her own family, a suitable inheritor of that value.

Leonard Bast returns briefly with his story of the adventure he has found in walking in the countryside at night. The Schlegels' concern for him becomes an ingredient of the next stage of the novel, which is the story of Margaret's relationship with Mr Wilcox. The analysis of the development of that relationship, and of the tension it causes between Margaret and her sister, is the subject of the central section of the novel. The association between Margaret and Mr Wilcox leads to a confrontation with Helen, who blames Mr Wilcox for giving bad advice to Leonard Bast. The revelation on that occasion that Mrs Bast has been Mr Wilcox's mistress does not lead to an immediate breach between Margaret and Mr Wilcox, but it marks the beginning of a slow recoil in Margaret's sympathies which ends in her reconciliation with Helen at Howards End. The final stage of Leonard Bast's story leads him to Howards End; during the journey he clarifies his understanding of his own life and purpose in a way that runs parallel to the experience of deeper self-awareness which Margaret has reached there. Leonard's journey ends in his death. This event introduces the final stage of the novel; it prevents the breach between Margaret and her husband, which had seemed unavoidable, and leads to a reconciliation between Margaret, Helen and Henry, which, however imperfect it may appear, seems to form the basis for a new family unit in the shelter of which new, and more successful, relationships may have the chance to develop.

Within this most general scheme of the pattern of the events of the novel, there are subordinate patterns of action which contribute significantly to the whole. The night Margaret spends with Helen at Howards End is the climax of a series of visits there, each of which has been too inconclusive to reveal the full significance of the house, although each has prepared for the final revelation of it. It is during these visits that we begin to see Margaret, not as a wife for Mr Wilcox but as a reincarnation, one might almost say, of the first Mrs Wilcox. Between Margaret's first and second visit to Howards End, Forster has placed her visit to Oniton. Oniton acts as a precursor for Howards End; it is the promise of which Howards End is the fulfilment. It is also the scene of the open breach between Margaret and Helen, and, as such, may be linked with a previous scene at Swanage when Helen is saddened by the news of her sister's engagement. Both series of scenes are links in the chain of events that leads Margaret from London to the countryside where she properly belongs.

If the novel had ended with Margaret's night at Howards End, it might have appeared that Helen's intransigent defence of Schlegel values had been right and that Margaret, after a temporary deviation, had returned to them. It is under Helen's influence, too, that Leonard Bast finds true personal values, even if he dies as he glimpses them. But the final chapter of the novel appears to suggest that Margaret, despite her failures, has travelled beyond Helen. Her search for a way of connecting Wilcox and Schlegel values has led to insights which transcend them. What these insights are may be impossible to state, except in religious terms, but they appear to distance Margaret from the simple optimism of the novel's ending, which it is left to Helen to express.

5.2 THE SYMBOLIC STRUCTURE

(a) Characterisation

Uncritically, we think of the events of the novel as happening to fictitious characters whom we treat as if they are real. Thus we may think of Margaret Schlegel as a serious-minded, well-to-do woman of the comfortably-off middle-class, who has a conscience about her wealth, which derives from the income of capital which has been prudently invested. She is interested in the social questions of the day, she is a liberal in politics and believes in the development of the individual, regardless of class. People tend to treat her with respect: she has a seriousness which gives her authority. She is the principal character in the novel; the decisions and discoveries which she makes during the course of it carry most of the weight of the meaning of the novel. She acts upon principle, but is flexible enough to modify her behaviour if she thinks it is mistaken. The deepest principle which she adheres to is always to respect the autonomy of others; the greatest test of this principle is when she is urged by Henry Wilcox to manipulate her sister, Helen, on the grounds that this will be for Helen's good. Her friendship with the Wilcoxes begins with Mrs Wilcox, but initially she fails to understand her. She is attracted to Henry Wilcox, after Mrs Wilcox's death, because he represents qualities which she takes to be complementary, and perhaps even superior, to those she has learned from her idealistic father. The Wilcoxes appear to make the money upon which the good things of her own life depend. In her view she has a duty to connect with, rather than to reject, that outer world of business and commerce. The main business of the novel is to gauge the soundness of this judgement. Through experience, she comes to see more clearly, what Mrs Wilcox has stood for; in that process she comes to resemble Mrs Wilcox herself. Margaret is almost always even-tempered, considerate, sensitive and thoughtful. It is through her that Forster's attachment to the values of the English countryside and the tradition of Romantic mysticism are most clearly expressed.

Helen Schlegel, her sister, is a less flexible character. Although she has many fine qualities of character and intelligence, she is more impulsive and more absolute than her sister. She has more faith in people than in places, but she is more partisan than her sister. After her first infatuation with the Wilcox family, as a result of which she falls in love with Paul, she refuses to believe that any connection with them can be good, though she is willing to accept Margaret's love for Henry in the final chapter of the novel. The strength of her social conscience is shown by her attachment to the Basts and the absoluteness of her attachment is demonstrated by her willingness to bear Leonard Bast's child. Wilfulness of this kind must throw doubt upon her judgement, but Forster treats her social transgression as a fortunate lapse which provides an optimistic ending for the novel. If there are ambiguities in her character, some of them must be attributed to the uses Forster makes of Helen in establishing some of the principal themes of the novel.

Their brother, Tibby, and their aunt, Mrs Munt, are more worldly characters. The negative aspects of Tibby's aestheticism have been discussed already: Mrs Munt's attachment to the values of the Schlegels is even less obvious – she is, after all, their mother's sister – and she remains instinctively and unashamedly materialistic. Although she likes to think of herself as a woman of culture, she is closer in spirit to the Wilcoxes than to the Schlegels. Indeed, she provides a useful, if unobtrusive, link between them.

The Wilcoxes are much less differentiated as a family. Henry and Charles Wilcox together represent the aggressively masculine ideal of certain Englishmen of the middle-class. They are acquisitive, eager to extend their own possessions and to justify their ambitions in the name of the greater glory of the Empire. Their aims of territorial expansion would rouse no sympathy now, but their entrepreneurial gifts would not be despised. Their defect is to think that there are no worlds other than those of business. This leads Henry Wilcox to believe that he can manage people as easily as he deals with objects. The understanding of the complex world of human feeling means little to him; indeed, he defends himself against it. It is only when Charles is jailed for manslaughter that his defences against emotion break down. But male Wilcoxes have no belief that people or places may be valued for their own sake; they have no sense that it is their duty to preserve the freedom of others.

Mrs Wilcox is, of course, wholly distinct from the men of her family. Essentially, she has married Mr Wilcox in order to preserve Howards End, the place she values above everything. Although she is not able to express her own sense of values, she clearly indicates that she is sceptical about any formulation of principles in verbal terms. Her knowledge, born of instinct and tradition, is of the heart. Her relationships with the rest of her family are loving but opaque. It is by her death that the notion of what she has stood for is released into the world of the novel: the inheritance which she has left to Margaret is a spiritual one. By a gradual process of concentration and reflection, Margaret comes to realise what it entails. Leonard and Jacky Bast complete the number of significant characters in the novel. They have often been criticised because of their unreality. Of the two, Jacky is treated the more savagely. The description of her in chapter six is harshly unsympathetic; perhaps it may be concluded that Forster was incapable of sympathising with a woman who represented aspects of female sexuality which he found threatening. Jacky, like Paul Wilcox, is not an independent character; each has a humble but necessary part to play in the action of the novel. Leonard Bast is a much more complex figure. He shares the ambitions of many working men of his time to participate fully in the educated life which their more fortunate contemporaries took for granted. Inevitably, such ambitions had a bookish seriousness which Forster finds limited. Leonard cannot distinguish between literature of the best quality and that which is second-rate. Besides, his motives may be suspect: does he admire the education of the middle-class for its own sake or as an avenue to material well-being? May it not be that Leonard, through no fault of his own, has been deprived of a culture of the senses which may well be superior to the mental culture he aspires to? Forster does not despise Leonard on grounds of snobbishness; if he makes fun of him, it is for pursuing suburban and domestic values and betraying the instinctual freedoms of the natural man for which Forster himself has such wistful sympathy.

Although we may be tempted to speak of these characters as real people, only a few of them possess the freedom which we take it for granted that we have in life. In particular, Margaret Schlegel is treated as a character who has freedom to choose and whose choices are significant for the action of the novel. Other characters are much more restricted by the part they have been given in the design of the novel as a whole. To a very large extent, their function is symbolic. They are part of the symbolic pattern of contrasts and gradations by which Schlegels are opposed to Wilcoxes, the world of nature to the world of business, or the human world to the infinite world of manifold significance, of which the human world is only part. It is for this reason that the characterisation of a novel must be considered as part of its total significance, to the structure of which it makes its own contribution.

(b) Places

As with persons, so with places: Forster carefully balances the settings of his characters against one another. London, of course, is a real place as are others mentioned in the book, but it is a reality filtered through the mind of the author, difficult to separate from the broader pattern of the imagery of the novel. King's Cross Station points to Infinity; St Paul's suggests disintegration. The London of the novel is formless and fluctuating, endlessly in process of renewal and decay, though the renewal is a kind of deterioration. Wickham Place, sheltered initially from these pressures, finally falls: 'Navvies came, and spilt it back into the grey' (Chapter 31). In Camelia Road, where Leonard Bast lives,

A block of flats, constructed with extreme cheapness, towered on either hand. Further down the road two more blocks were being built, and beyond these an old house was being demolished to accommodate another pair. (Chapter 6)

London is an advancing tide which menaces the rest of the country, eroding it physically and sapping the vitality of smaller communities.

Hilton is a village within easy reach of London, and convenient for the purposes of businessmen like Charles Wilcox. It owes its existence to traffic along the Great North Road in the days before the motor car. Now, a residential town, it was being rebuilt according to the taste of the commuter, but 'the stream of residences that was thickening up' there had not entirely obliterated the landscape, in particular the Six Hills under which soldiers of the Danish invasions in the tenth century lay buried, and beyond which could be seen meadow and wood.

Howards End, the house which had belonged to Mrs Wilcox's family, lies near to Hilton. It is as yet untouched by the encroachment of the metropolis. It is an old brick-built farm house, set in its own grounds with a vine and a wych-elm growing nearby. Although Margaret is unaware of the fact, Howards End is the object of her quest for permanent values. Its attractiveness is established from the first page of the novel. Mrs Wilcox's deep sense of its value is conveyed to Margaret during their Christmas shopping expedition in Chapter 10. Mrs Wilcox instinctively believes that Margaret is the kind of person to whom Howards End should belong. The events of the novel show how this intuition is realised. Howards End, of course, is not simply a place: it stands for the idea of pre-industrial England, an idealised agricultural paradise of social harmony, health and contentment.

Oniton, which Forster based on the town of Clun on the Welsh border not far from Shrewsbury, has an important part to play in the novel because it is the place where Margaret first realises that life in the country has special virtues which she wishes to foster. Surrounded by hills and rivers, 'the house was insignificant but the prospect from it would be an eternal joy'. The possibility of 'eternal joy' is destroyed by the sad human events that take place at Oniton, but it is a stage on the way to Howards End.

Swanage is the home of Mrs Munt, aunt of Margaret and Helen. It is the scene of one of the most often quoted episodes in the novel (Chapter 19). Mrs Munt shares some of the spirit of the Wilcoxes: she is snobbish and limited. For her the commercial development of Swanage is a matter for pride. Swanage represents English reasonableness, English conventionality; yet from a few miles beyond it, all England – its wildness and passionate romanticism – can be discovered.

(c) Imagery
One of the most striking uses of imagery in *Howards End* is the contrast Forster draws between sea and river. In Chapter 2 Wickham

Place is described as 'a backwater, or rather . . . an estuary, whose water flowed in from the invisible sea, and ebbed into a profound silence while the waves without were still beating.' In Chapter 13 the Schlegel household is 'still swimming gracefully on the grey tides of London', and John Ruskin, in the passage from *The Stones of Venice* which Leonard reads in Chapter 6, glides 'over the whispering lagoons' of Venice, itself a city built previously on the sea. In Chapter 13 London itself 'rose and fell in a continual flux'. At the end of Chapter 15, as Margaret watches the ebbing of the tide on the Thames the 'continual flux' is found in 'the hearts of men' themselves. At Howards End, in Chapter 24, 'the sense of flux which had haunted [Margaret] all the year disappeared for a time'. London is seen as a tide which threatens the beauty and integrity of rural values. In Chapter 19 the tides are the seas which swirl round England, which is seen here (and in Chapter 11) as an ocean-going vessel bound with its company for some unknown destination. Presumably it is as members of this national crew that the Wilcoxes are described as seeming 'to have their hands on all the ropes'. The implications of this sea-imagery are threatening and destructive.

In contrast, rivers provide the novel with some of its most appealing imagery. Perhaps the first mention of a river is in Chapter 9 where Margaret commends the beautiful view of the Oder at Stettin and tells Mrs Wilcox that she

> would love the Oder. The river, or rather rivers – there seem to be dozens of them – are intense blue, and the plain they run through an intensest green.

Her next mention of rivers is disparaging. In the context of her engagement to Henry Wilcox in Chapter 20 she says,

> I hate this continual flux of London. It is an epitome of us at our worst – eternal formlessness; all the qualities, good, bad, and indifferent, streaming away – streaming, streaming forever. That's why I dread it so. I mistrust rivers, even in scenery. Now the sea –

Her commendation of the sea (if that is what she had in mind) remains unspoken. But Forster's development of river symbolism from this point suggests that Margaret has been mistaken. At Oniton in Chapter 25 'a little river whispered, full of messages from the west' – from Celtic Wales. Leonard and Helen hear 'the murmurings of the river' before, presumably, they make love at Oniton. In the night of Margaret and Helen's stay at Howards End 'the present flowed by them like a stream'. In Chapter 19 rivers are celebrated as part of the view worth showing to a foreigner; in Chapter 23 they are described as dishevelled nymphs averting their eyes from the smoke of London. There is nothing logical or natural about the contrast Forster draws between rivers and sea: he has chosen to select positive associations for one, negative associations for the other. His references to rivers are part of his reliance on the values of the countryside; his references to sea spring from associations of erosion and changeableness.

Other examples of natural imagery worth mentioning are the wych-elm and the vine at Howards End and, perhaps, the sun and moon. The first clearly stands for all the mystical and superstitious properties which cluster round the house, which itself stands for England. Together, the wych-elm and the vine signify the ideal of comradeship, more potent in this novel than that of marriage or of sexual love. Alone, the vine (in Chapter 35) serves as an appropriately fruitful frame for Helen who is 'with child'. The sun is associated briefly with the love which Margaret feels for Henry after he has asked her to marry him. But 'the central radiance' which fills her with joy at that time alters after Henry's collapse to something more remote and more protective. The moon, on the other hand, presides over her night with Helen at Howards End, and becomes for Leonard Bast a symbol for unity, for the assimilation of things that are disparate, as 'Sea of Serenity, Sea of Tranquillity, Ocean of Lunar Storms, merged into one lucent drop, itself to slip into the sempiternal dawn' (Chapter 41). The capacity to see contraries and opposites as part of a larger unity, in which contradictions are illusory, is perhaps the virtue which sends Leonard in search, not of Helen, but of Margaret.

One final image which is worth mentioning is the fortress or bastion or blank wall, which Forster makes of Henry Wilcox's forehead, and behind which he protects himself until the last paragraph of the penultimate chapter of the novel.

(d) Thematic contrasts

Much of the argument of *Howards End* is carried in a series of contrasts which Forster draws between what is known and what is unknown, what is seen and what is unseen. One set of these contrasts refers to a division between the imperfect world of time and a transcendent, but unknowable, eternal world; another refers to oppositions within the lower world itself. So, 'the visible and the invisible', 'the seen and the unseen' are phrases which refer to the first of these; 'the prose and the passion', 'the beast and the monk', 'the inner and the outer life' refer to the second. As the epigraph of the novel – 'only connect' – implies, *Howards End* is a sustained investigation into the relationships that may be made between the oppositions within the human world and – less obviously perhaps – between the two worlds themselves. Margaret puts her own idea of the connection thus in Chapter 22:

> Only connect! That was the whole of her sermon. Only connect the prose and the passion, and both will be exalted, and human love will be seen at its height. Live in fragments no longer. Only connect, and the beast and the monk, robbed of isolation that is life to either, will die.

Her project to rescue the soul of Henry and integrate his aggressive, self-confident outer attitude with the 'incomplete asceticism' of his inner life is admirable, and comparable to her parallel aim of integrating her own world of culture with the world of business and money-making. It is not obvious, however, that these aims further the contact between the everyday world and the world of infinity. Moreover, it is not clear from the action of the novel that they succeed.

Leonard Bast also lives in a divided world in which his aspirations to culture are at odds with his poverty. He prefers to keep his acquaintance with the Schlegels separate from his life at work or at home. But the divisions between money and culture, which confuse and depress him, are transcended by the insight he gains at the end of life into values which are superior to both of them.

Forster was a student of Greek literature and was familiar with the 'two-world' view of the Greek philosopher, Plato (c.427 – c.347 BC). Plato made a sharp division between the everyday world of time and chance and an eternal world of absolute values. Christian theologians incorporated ideas of this kind into their picture of the world. Human time was contrasted with eternity, human imperfection with divine perfection. Forster's contrast of the Visible and the Invisible, the Seen and the Unseen, seems nearer the first of these than the second. Helen Schlegel believes in a world of absolute values, and it is one of Margaret's early beliefs that 'any human being lies nearer to the unseen than any organization'. The question for the reader must be, however, whether Forster's Infinity, his world of the 'unseen' and the 'invisible' is not something more mysterious and elusive than the Platonic world of absolute value. His references to it are often teasing and vague, but it seems to lie in a territory shared by modern occultism and ancient folk-magic, about whose validity the reader may have legitimate doubts.

(e) Some key words and phrases

We have already noticed how the word 'grey' is frequently used in the novel to suggest the dull, featureless, undifferentiated substance out of which ordinary life – the life of the lower world of every day – is composed. Forster has woven his use of the word so skilfully into the fabric of his novel that his repetition of it never obtrudes, never seems the merely mechanical expression of a symbolic effect. Another such word, less often used, is 'joy', which means the most vivid awareness of being alive, our keenest and purest sense of life. Sometimes this might be associated with sex, or with love, or with some profound sense of what life's purpose is. Another frequently repeated word is 'collide' or 'collision', terms which Forster uses when he wants to refer to that quality of randomness which is such an inescapable feature of human life. It expresses a concept which is opposed to purposiveness – and yet, as Forster says of Helen's passing feeling for Paul, 'by collisions of this trivial sort the doors of heaven may be shaken open'. Chance and randomness may in some mysterious way be connected with what endures.

'Only connect', the phrase which Forster uses as the epigraph to the novel, is not a phrase which he repeats. Its appearance in Chapter 22 is a response evoked by contrasts and oppositions which have been established in earlier chapters and it is foreshadowed by Margaret's advice to Helen in chapter 12,

> 'Don't brood too much . . . on the superiority of the unseen to the seen . . . Our business is not to contrast the two but to reconcile them'.

More often repeated are the phrases 'panic and emptiness' and 'telegrams and anger' which Helen applies to the inner and outer worlds of the Wilcoxes, to their inability to deal with personal relationships or with the external world except by force of will. To the Schlegels, initially at any rate, it is the Wilcoxes who have 'their hands on all the ropes', but Leonard Bast applies the phrase to the Schlegels themselves. In fact, the phrase is ironical, since the kind of control it implies over the difficulties of life is neither possible nor even, perhaps, desirable. One final phrase, 'to see life steadily and see it whole', – borrowed from a poem by Matthew Arnold (1822–88) – is repeated many times. Arnold used it to express the comprehensive, classical vision of the Greek dramatist, Sophocles. Forster adapts it to his own purposes. As he says of Margaret:

> it is impossible to see modern life steadily and whole, and she had chosen to see it whole. Mr Wilcox saw it steadily.

Leonard Bast thinks that 'to see life steadily and to see it whole was not for the likes of him'. But it may be argued that Leonard, like Margaret, comes to see it whole. Helen sees life steadily: her fierce idealism complements Mr Wilcox's materialism.

(f) Narrative voice

From the first throwaway sentence – 'One may as well begin with Helen's letters to her sister' – to the impassioned prose of Chapter 19 and elsewhere, Forster displays an extraordinary range of tone. For most of the novel, the voice of the narrator is easy and balanced. It is lucid but conversational, though the conversation is that of an assured and civilised gentleman, clear-sighted, meditative, and shrewd. The narrative voice is intimate, inviting the reader to follow – and possibly disagree with – the judgements which it makes on the events which it records. Its essential mode is appraisal; it weighs and balances, summing up with the pithy gravity of eighteenth-century prose. Of Tibby, it says (in Chapter 30)

> Tibby neither wished to strengthen the position of the rich nor to improve that of the poor, and so was well content to watch the elms nodding behind the mildly embattled parapets of Magdalen. There are worse lives. Though selfish, he was never cruel; though affected in manner, he never posed.

It is easy to see the balanced antitheses of these sentences, but one might easily miss the irony in that almost self-contradictory 'mildly embattled', as if the battles engaged in at Oxford were neither strenuous nor momentous. And the commendation of his life is double-edged: if Tibby has no positive vices, his virtues are negative – only his affectation is sincere. Forster stresses the qualities he can praise, but the qualifying clauses are damning.

There is nothing uniform, though, about the narrative voice of *Howards End*; it is composed of many voices, one layered upon the other. Detached irony may give place to a deeply-engaged, almost rhapsodic commitment to values which, it is implied, only imagination can grasp. Behind apparently neutral descriptive statements, the reader is aware of a sharply observant narrative presence which invites the reader to judge, even if it makes no comment. As Tibby for example, watches Helen in tears, the narrator watches Tibby:

> He had known her hysterical – it was one of her aspects with which he had no concern – and yet these tears touched him as something unusual. They were nearer the things that did concern him, such as music. He laid down his knife and looked at her curiously. Then, as she continued to sob, he went on with his lunch.

The narrator expects that the reader will not approve of Tibby. Most people are moved by the troubles of others; they do not need to think of music to pay attention to the sound of crying. Tibby's calm is chilling and Forster's sentences mimic it so accurately – the inter-rupted act of eating, the registered, but disregarded sob, the look, the continued lunch – that the reader is forced to respond to the report as he would to the event itself. And Forster has no doubt what the response would be.

(g) Point of view
It is this capacity for mimicry, perhaps, which accounts for one of the most striking characteristics of the novel's technique. Although much of the novel is narrated from the point of view of a detached, ironic observer, who follows the actions he reports with a probing, deli-berate intelligence, his capacity for sympathetic mimicry enables him from time to time to come so close to one of the characters that he is able to see events from that character's point of view. Closeness, of course, implies sympathy: Forster is closest to Margaret, but as the previous section demonstrates, he knows what is like to be Tibby. In Chapter 11 we even find him slipping into the voice of Mr Wilcox as he thinks about his dead wife:

> He remembered his wife's even goodness during thirty years. Not anything in detail – not courtship or early raptures – but just the unvarying virtue, that seemed to him a woman's noblest quality. So many women are capricious, breaking into odd flaws of passion or frivolity. Not so his wife. Year after year, summer and winter, as bride and mother, she had been the same, he had always trusted her. Her tenderness! Her innocence! The wonderful innocence that was hers by the gift of God.

It is noticeable how this passage, which begins as a report about the working of Mr Wilcox's mind – his act of remembering – slips easily into words which might easily be the content of that mental process. The narrator has suspended judgement; he simply allows words that could easily have been Mr Wilcox's to pass across the page, for the moment almost becoming Mr Wilcox. Yet the reader is not allowed to suspend judgement: what kind of picture of Mrs Wilcox are we being given? Do these words characterise her truly, or are they representative of the quality of her husband's thinking? Perhaps the answer is that the truth to which they point is not understood by Mr Wilcox and is wholly alien to his ways of thinking.

(h) Free indirect speech
When a narrator offers a representation of the thoughts of one of his characters, not as directly uttered nor as objectively reported, but as they might arise spontaneously in his or her mind, the author is using what is often called 'free indirect speech'. Essentially this means that the speech is in the third person and the past tense, but it is not tied to

the narrative by words such as 'that' or 'whether' or 'if'. Consider Chapter 22 where Margaret hopes that she will be able to help Mr Wilcox to love:

> It did not seem so difficult. She need trouble him with no gift of her own. She would only point out the salvation that was latent hin his own soul, and in the soul of every man. Only connect! That was the whole of her sermon. Only connect the prose and the passion, and both will be exalted, and human love will be seen at its height. Live in fragments no longer. Only connect, and the beast and the monk, robbed of the isolation that is life to either, will die.

The passage is written from Margaret's point of view. It begins in the past tense, as if Margaret is looking back on the sequence of her own thoughts which are being reported by the narrator. When the central phrase, 'only connect', is reached, it is left to float freely, as if it has just burst into her mind. For a moment the narrator intervenes to remind us that these are Margaret's words, but in the next sentence the words are again Margaret's, as she develops her thought. Now they are direct imperatives: she has found a maxim on which she means to act, and she looks forward to the effects of living by it. By using this method of presenting Margaret's thoughts, Forster is able to render them with vivid immediacy. He is also able to leave the responsibility for them entirely with Margaret. A careless reader might easily take them for a comment by the narrator. Clearly they are not, but is it entirely clear how far Margaret's belief is endorsed by the author?

6 SPECIMEN PASSAGE
AND COMMENTARY

6.1 SPECIMEN PASSAGE

The passage chosen for commentary consists of the final paragraphs of Chapter 27, the dialogue between Helen Schlegel and Leonard Bast which precedes their night together in a hotel at Oniton:

> 'We are all in a mist – I know, but I can help you this far – men like the Wilcoxes are deeper in the mist than any. Sane, sound Englishmen! Building up empires, levelling all the world into what they call common sense. But mention Death to them and they're offended, because Death's really Imperial, and He cries out against them for ever'.
> 'I am as afraid of Death as anyone'.
> 'But not of the idea of Death'.
> 'But what is the difference?'
> 'Infinite difference', said Helen, more gravely than before.
>
> Leonard looked at her wondering, and had the sense of great things sweeping out of the shrouded night. But he could not receive them, because his heart was still full of little things. As the lost umbrella had spoilt the concert at Queen's Hall, so the lost situation was obscuring the diviner harmonies now. Death, Life and Materialism were fine words, but would Mr Wilcox take him on as a clerk? Talk as one would, Mr Wilcox was king of this world, the superman, with his own morality, whose head remained in the clouds.
>
> 'I must be stupid', he said apologetically.
>
> While to Helen the paradox became clearer and clearer. 'Death destroys a man; the idea of Death saves him'. Behind the coffins and the skeletons that stay the vulgar mind lies something so

immense that all that is great in us responds to it. Men of the world may recoil from the charnel-house that they will one day enter, but Love knows better. Death is his foe, but not his peer, and in their age-long struggle the thews of Love have been strengthened, and his vision cleared, until there is no one who can stand against him.

'So never give in', continued the girl, and restated again and again the vague yet convincing plea that the Invisible lodges against the Visible. Her excitement grew as she tried to cut the rope that fastened Leonard to the earth. Woven of bitter experience, it resisted her. Presently the waitress entered and gave her a letter from Margaret. Another note, addressed to Leonard, was inside. They read them, listening to the murmurings of the river.

6.2 COMMENTARY

Consideration of this passage may help the reader to think about Helen. Readers and critics are apt to take her at Forster's valuation – that is, according to the judgement expressed by the narrator, particularly at the end of Chapter 4, where we are told that she 'advanced along the same lines [as Margaret], though with a more irresponsible tread'. And later, 'the younger was rather apt to entice people, and, in enticing them, to be herself enticed'. And yet in the following chapter, Helen is given the extended meditation on Beethoven's Fifth Symphony, which may be in accordance with a strain of wildness in her imagination, but which is nowhere repudiated by the author – which remains, indeed, a primary insight into the nature of the universe which Forster has created in *Howards End*.

This passage is equally imaginative, equally metaphysical. It is a meditation on the way human beings come to know what kind of things are morally valuable. The way to such knowledge, Helen argues, is by a full appreciation of the absolutely destructive power of Death. In the darkness of that knowledge, people may see more clearly what matters to them, what they would most miss if the world were destroyed.

The first paragraph of the passage – Helen's first speech – links with many other passages in the novel. The account we are given in Chapter 4 of the reasons for Ernst Schlegel's departure from Germany clearly establishes a central position taken up by the novel as a whole about the extension of national sovereignty, and about increases in armaments. The same points are made in Chapter 17. Only death has the right to be called Emperor. When Helen speaks of the 'infinite difference' between the brute fact of Death and the idea of Death, she is using a serious pun. Yes, the difference between these concepts is very great, but, more significantly, the idea of Death carries with it – logically implies, she seems to argue – the idea of Infinity. Immediately, we are reminded, surely, of the chilling scene in the graveyard at Hilton (in Chapter 11) where the evocation of the silence and emptiness of the scene is succeeded by the metaphor of the church seen as a ship, high-prowed, steering with all its company towards infinity. So we may add to the list of linked opposites that we have found in the novel the pairing Death/Infinity, which may appear oppposed but are in fact connected.

Nothing in the narrative suggests that Leonard is wrong to have 'the sense of great things sweeping out of the shrouded night'. It is precisely out of such a darkness that the things he holds dearest should appear. (Compare, in Chapter 10, Margaret's apprehension of 'the invisible' – the truth about Mrs Wilcox – after the darkness of the failure of their Christmas shopping expedition.) But Leonard cannot move towards 'things', since he remains at the level of 'words'. Notice how the narrator's commentary takes on the accents of Leonard himself, until it merges with his belief that, in some way that reminds him dimly of the German philosopher Nietzsche, Mr Wilcox has become a law unto himself and that, as 'the superman', what he wills is right. The words he speaks – 'I must be stupid'–are meant as an apology for not understanding Helen, but we can see them as a comment (unintended by Leonard, but not by Forster) on his opinion of Mr Wilcox. As Helen's perceptions grow clearer, the commentator expands them in language which is nearer to the seventeenth than to the twentieth century. Expressions such as 'stay', 'charnel-house', 'thews' and 'lodge against' lend an archaic or poetic flavour to the passage. 'Stay' means 'to keep immovable', 'to delay', 'to arrest the attention of'; 'thews' means 'vigour', 'strength' but is not a word used much in modern English unless in the expression 'thew and sinew'; 'lodges against' means 'to deposit in court a formal statement (of complaint, or objection)'. Forster's use of this slightly unusual vocabulary gives the passage a resonance and intensity which is intended to convey to the reader the seriousness and solemnity of the opinion being expressed here – which seems no longer merely Helen's opinion but one which has been taken over and restated by the narrator himself. Some readers may think that the language does not in fact do this: Forster links the adjectives 'vague' and 'convincing', it may be argued, in a vain attempt to assert significance without committing himself to anything. It is impressive to talk of the battle between Love and Death – but what kind of love is intended? Is it the sexual love we hear of in Chapter 18 and which seems to be referred to at the beginning of Chapter 20, where the struggle between Love and Death seems to be alluded to for the first time? Is it the quasi-maternal love which Margaret seems to conceive for Henry Wilcox at the end of chapter 43? Or is it some more general love of the Good? The word is often used in *Howards End* – never more crucially than in the final chapter where Margaret and Helen disagree about its value – but is it quite clear what it means?

The reader's attention has been drawn to the way in which the and the ornateness of the prose is simplified to the colloquial, 'So characters. Here, the opposite happens: Helen's opinions are taken up, and amplified by the narrator, who in turn gives way to Helen, and the ornateness of the prose is simplified to the colloquial, 'So never give in'. In calling her 'the girl' Forster repeats an affectionate term, which he used in Chapter 5, when Helen saw the goblins in Beethoven's Fifth Symphony. He supports her restatement of 'the vague yet convincing plea the Invisible lodges against the Invisible'. But his tone shifts as he dissociates himself from the excesses of her idealism. Forster deflates his own rhetoric, by a reference to Leonard which is not so much a joke as a wry recognition that Leonard's resistance to her enthusiasm is rooted in lived experience. But Helen's attempt 'to cut the rope that fastened Leonard to earth' – which the narrator smiles at, using a metaphor which might suggest Leonard is a passenger in a hot-air balloon – is not essentially different from the narrator's implied wish that 'little things' had not prevented Leonard from seeing 'great things sweeping out of the shrouded night'. On the other hand, what Helen offers Leonard is words, whereas it has already been established that Leonard's only hope for a fuller life lies in a closer contact with the earth. Messages of a literal kind appear from Margaret, but it is to the 'murmurings' of the river that Leonard and Helen are listening as the passage ends. It is the river which flows through Oniton bringing messages of the infinite and the unseen from the hills of Wales.

7 CRITICAL RECEPTION

Howards End was published in 1910. Its early reviewers were in general enthusiastic about Forster's progress. One review called it 'the year's best novel', and more than one spoke of its combination of persuasive generalisation and sharply observed surface detail. There were some dissenting voices about the probability of character and event, and some reviewers believed that the novel was spoiled by melodrama and by the author's willingness to sacrifice probability to the demands of the design of his novel. The strongest objections were to the probability of Helen's love affair with Leonard Bast, though one reviewer was equally shocked by Margaret's marriage to Mr Wilcox. The same reviewer believed that the finer feelings of Margaret Schlegel should not have been sacrificed in favour of enlarging her sympathies which the Wilcoxes: 'we cannot admit that what is bad ought to be loved'. (unsigned review, *Athenaeum*, 3 December 1910). This reviewer might have agreed with D. H. Lawrence, who wrote to Forster in 1915, 'broken Henry's (sic) remain Henry's as I know to my cost' and later, 'I think you *did* make a nearly deadly mistake glorifying those business people in *Howards End*. Business is no good'. Another friend of Forster's however, A. C. Benson, 'took the book rather to be a study of the immense strength of sturdy, conventional humanity'. R. A. Scott-James in the *Daily News* saw Charles and Helen as antithetical figures representing the extremes of Wilcox brutality and Schlegel sloppiness: Margaret 'has her feet at least firmly planted on the earth, and she is able to make a success of marriage with Henry Wilcox' and the reviewer confirmed his account by quoting the 'Only connect' passage in Chapter 22. Many reviewers commented on the extraordinary power of Forster's evocation of the spirit of place. The characterisation was praised, in particular that of Mrs Wilcox, though an anonymous reviewer in the *Westminster Gazette* felt that her development into a kind of mystical 'over-soul' had not been properly prepared for. In some quarters there was an uneasy suspicion that the book constituted an attack on the English middle classes, despite equally strong feelings elsewhere that it was precisely this class which was being admired for having made England what it is.

In general, R. A. Scott-James's account of the novel remained the standard view for many years, even although some doubts were expressed about the persuasiveness of Margaret's final reconciliation of Schlegel and Wilcox values. In 1944 Lionel Trilling saw *Howards End* as Forster's masterpiece. Its theme, according to him, is an internal conflict within the middle class: its aim to answer the question, 'Who shall inherit England?' For Trilling, the Schlegel sisters represent the intellectual class, dependent on money made by the Wilcoxes: they have a paternalistic attitude towards their social inferiors. Helen and Margaret have both fallen in love with the masculinity of the Wilcoxes, which proves defective. The only other man in the novel, Leonard Bast, fails because he has pursued a false goal of aesthetic culture. What is left is the feminine principle in the person of Margaret and Helen. Not only has the Wilcox pragmatism been defeated but the vigilant reasonableness represented by the Schlegels' father has also disappeared. Whether Margaret's feminine intuition, handed down from Ruth Wilcox, is an improvement on this latter quality remains an open question. The son of Leonard Bast and Helen symbolises the 'connection' which Margaret has achieved, but what its nature is Trilling leaves unclear. The child's role as inheritor remains ambiguous and not entirely optimistic. Trilling's account of the novel, though general, is penetrating and challenging.

In 1952, F. R. Leavis in *The Common Pursuit* complained about the unreality of *Howards End*: we could not believe in the marriage of Margaret and Mr Wilcox nor in the affair of Helen and Leonard Bast. Leavis believed that Forster did not understand people like Leonard. He thought the novel depended too much on symbols. We are not encouraged to understand the value attached to Howards End, because no detailed account is given of the way of life it represents. In place of specific detail, Forster tries to use an impure prose-poetry to achieve effects that, in Leavis's view, can only be achieved by the ordered imaginative representation of reality. Leavis's criticism of *Howards End* rests on an assumption about the techniques which are appropriate to the novelist and about the relationships which should exist between fiction and reality.

In his study of the novel in *The Novels of E. M. Forster* (1957) James McConkey stresses 'the mysterious power of place'. The stability and rootedness of Howards End is contrasted with a nomadic civilisation, associated with the Wilcoxes. The novel may be seen as a voyage towards Howards End. Margaret, the captain of the ship, is aided by the spiritual presence of Mrs Wilcox. McConkey discusses the water imagery which abounds in the novel; he notes the symbolic means by which Forster links Margaret and Mrs Wilcox. In McConkey's view *Howards End* suffers because there is too close a relationship between Margaret, who is intended to reconcile and connect, and the narrative voice which is essentially solitary and detached. As the novel progresses, margaret's detachment becomes more pronounced; it is Helen and her child who are left to be the channel of future events.

While McConkey's book is primarily an analysis of Forster's literary technique, Frederick Crews in *E. M. Forster: the perils of humanism* (1962) sets his discussion of the novel in the context of an account of late nineteenth-century liberal opinion. Crews suggests that one difficulty about the book is that, though it contains the sharpest exposure of aggressive capitalism dominant in the late nineteenth century, Forster appears to wish us to be sympathetic towards it. He notes the significance of Howards End as a value in the novel, and the connection between Mrs Wilcox and Margaret. He accepts the polarisation of Helen Schlegel and Charles Wilcox, seeing Margaret as the central character who achieves a balance by exploring the opposed values which they represent. Crews sees Margaret's many-sided capacity for connection as the key to the meaning of the novel. Yet he is not convinced by his own analysis. He suggests that Forster's aim was to present Margaret in this way but it remains a diagram only: the dark forces of reality have been too much for Forster's reconciling ideal.

John Beer, in *The Achievement of E. M. Forster* (1963) stresses the value given to the spirit of place, contrasting the stability of Howards End with the changeableness of London. He plays down the 'moments of vision' in the novel, preferring to stress Margaret's capacity to love Henry Wilcox, though her love does not include suburbanism or the sordidness represented by the Basts. For Mr Beer, the Basts are not only unconvincing as examples of a social type, they are people who cannot be reached by any true conception of culture. The ending of the novel presents the triumph of a limited good which succeeds by excluding the darker elements of the material it has assembled. Thus it is less inclusive, and therefore less successful, than the more comprehensive *A Passage to India* which was to follow it.

In an essay published in *Forster: a collection of critical essays*, edited by himself (1966), Malcolm Bradbury takes a different view. He considers that *Howards End* fails because Forster has not been able to integrate the symbolic and the realistic modes of writing fiction. He suggests that *Howards End* is more ironic than has been supposed and that much of the irony is self-directed. The irony that Bradbury detects is not a matter of tone or style; it rests in the contrasts between the optimistic conclusion of the novel, on the one hand, with which Bradbury associates both Margaret Schlegel and the supporting voice of the narrator and, on the other, the destructive forces of history which the novel describes. Bradbury argues that at the end of the novel, Forster means us to realise that what Margaret thinks of as a success – her move to Howards End – is only the temporary solution to historical and philosophical problems which are more complex than agrarian liberalism can deal with. Since the novel has no other solution to offer, its conclusion is an ironic comment on Forster's own belief.

In an extended study of the novel (*E. M. Forster's* HOWARDS END: *Fiction as History* (1977) Peter Widdowson considers the novel as an expression of the conflicts and ambiguities of liberal humanism in the early twentieth century. Widdowson asserts that the conceptual foundations of this world were breaking up because of the recognition that the claims of the individual were subordinate to those of the community. The fictional mode of realism which had expressed a confident bourgeois ideology no longer sufficed to express the internal conflicts of that system. Widdowson takes the theme of the novel to be 'money and its relationship to the life of liberal-humanist values'. He assumes that Margaret is the mouthpiece for Forster's own attitudes, but concedes that she makes many false starts and 'comes close to betraying her own values'. In choosing the son of Helen and Leonard Bast as the future inheritor of Howards End, Forster shows that money and culture in combination are not enough. Leonard carries the buried vitality of an uprooted class which, returned to its rural setting, may flourish again, 'given money and the 'life of values'.'

Widdowson believes, however, that Forster's picture of 'liberal England' is false, because he does not give enough weight to the forces which threaten it. Forster is too intent to prove a case–that Howards End shall survive and the right people shall inherit England. He fails to supply the reader with enough corroborative detail to convince him that his social analysis is sound. Forster knows that his Utopian vision of a continuing rural England is no longer tenable, but he persists in creating a work of fiction which attempts to make it appear true.

Readers will want to make up their own minds, but some of the main points of critical disagreement have emerged from this review of some informed discussions of the novel. Does the final chapter of the novel provide it with a satisfactory ending? Is a writer justified in mixing symbolic and realistic modes of writing? How accurate, and how fair, is Forster's representation of Leonard Bast and Jacky? To what extent is Margaret Schlegel a 'mouthpiece' for a Forster's own views? What kind of role is given to the narrator? Is Forster's irony mainly a matter of theme and plot, or does it operate more subtly and more pervasively in the prose style of the novel itself? Is the epigraph 'Only connect' a recommendation, or is it, perhaps, the expression of a rather tentative hope? Whatever answers may be given to them, or whatever further questions may be raised, *Howards End* remains a subtle and intricately constructed novel which requires careful reading.

REVISION QUESTIONS

1. What qualities are represented by (a) the Schlegels, (b) the Wilcoxes?

2. In what ways does Forster link the events of contemporary history to the events of his novel?

3. What differences does Forster draw between Helen and Margaret Wilcox?

4. How do you think these differences in character between the sisters affect the course of the novel?

5. What function does Tibby, their brother, play in the pattern of the novel?

6. When, in your view, is the fact of Mrs Wilcox's special significance as a character in the novel established in the novel? By what means does Forster make this point?

7. How successful do you think Forster has been in creating the characters of Leonard and Jacky Bast? Does his success or failure affect their value as elements in the design of the novel as a whole?

8. In what ways does Leonard Bast develop as a character?

9. Helen Schlegel contributes more to the argument of the novel than to its action. Do you agree?

10. What evidence would you produce to support the view that *Howards End* is a critical examination of Margaret Schlegel's behaviour and attitudes rather than an endorsement of them.

11. In what way do you think that the epigraph 'only connect' is related to the action of the novel?

12. How far do you think Forster supports Margaret's opinion that the essential basis of social life is economic?

13. It is clear enough why Helen gives money to Leonard Bast but why does Forster make Margaret give away her money in the last chapter of the novel?

14. What opinion do you have on the passages of 'prose poetry' which can be found in, for example, Chapters 19 and 22? Does writing of this kind require special justification? Can you offer arguments for or against it?

15. The view of *Howards End* offered here has frequently drawn attention to the religious or mystical dimension of the novel? Discuss whether this dimension (a) exists, (b) has the significance ascribed to it, (c) is made plausible by Forster.

16. Do you believe the final chapter of the novel brings it to a satisfactory conclusion? Defend your point of view.

17. Do you think that Forster's use of terms such as 'the invisible', 'the unseen', 'Infinity' and so on is carelessly obscure, or can his vagueness be justified?

18. Do you think it is a valid criticism of the novel that Forster has failed to give a sufficiently explicit account of the ways of life represented by Howards End, on which he sets such a high value?

FURTHER READING

Text
The best text of the novel is published as volume 4 of The Abinger Edition of E. M. Forster, edited by Oliver Stallybrass (London, 1973). A paperback edition of it is published by Penguin Books, Harmondsworth, 1984.

Biographical
P. N. Furbank, *E. M. Forster: A Life*, 2 vols (London, 1977).
Mary Lago and P. N. Furbank (eds), *Selected Letters of E. M. Forster*, Vol. 1 (London, 1983).

Critical
John Beer, *The Achievement of E. M. Forster* (London, 1962).
Frederick Crews, *E. M. Forster: the Perils of Humanism* (Princeton, 1962).
K. W. Gransden, *E. M. Forster* (London, 1962).
F. R. Leavis, 'E. M. Forster', in *The Common Pursuit* (London, 1952).
James McConkey, *The Novels of E. M. Forster* (New York, 1957).
Lionel Trilling, *E. M. Forster* (London, 1944; revised edition 1967).
Peter Widdowson, *E. M. Forster's 'Howards End'* (London, 1977).

Mastering English Literature
Richard Gill

Mastering English Literature will help readers both to enjoy English Literature and to be successful in 'O' levels, 'A' levels and other public exams. It is an introduction to the study of poetry, novels and drama which helps the reader in four ways – by providing ways of approaching literature, by giving examples and practice exercises; by offering hints on how to write about literature, and by the author's own evident enthusiasm for the subject. With extracts from more than 200 texts, this is an enjoyable account of how to get the maximum satisfaction out of reading, whether it be for formal examinations or simply for pleasure.

Work Out English Literature ('A' level)
S.H. Burton

This book familiarises 'A' level English Literature candidates with every kind of test which they are likely to encounter. Suggested answers are worked out step by step and accompanied by full author's commentary. The book helps students to clarify their aims and establish techniques and standards so that they can make appropriate responses to similar questions when the examination pressures are on. It opens up fresh ways of looking at the full range of set texts, authors and critical judgements and motivates students to know more of these matters.